C. H. Spurgeon

Spurgeon's Sermons
on
Great Prayers
of the Bible

CHARLES HADDON SPURGEON

kregel
PUBLICATIONS

Grand Rapids, MI 49501

Spurgeon's Sermons on Great Prayers of the Bible
by Charles H. Spurgeon

© 1995 by Kregel Publications

Published by Kregel Publications, a division of Kregel, Inc.,
P. O. Box 2607, Grand Rapids, MI 49501. Kregel
Publications provides trusted, biblical publications for
Christian growth and service. Your comments and sugges-
tions are valued.

Cover artwork: Don Ellens
Cover and book design: Alan G. Hartman

Library of Congress Cataloging-in-Publication Data

Spurgeon, C. H. (Charles Haddon), 1834–1892.
  [Sermons on prayer]
  Spurgeon's sermons on great prayers of the bible /
by Charles H. Spurgeon.
        p.   cm.—(C. H. Spurgeon sermon series)
  1. Prayer—Christianity—Sermons. 2. Sermons,
English. 3. Baptists—Sermons. I. Title.
II. Series: Spurgeon, C. H. (Charles Haddon),
1834–1892. C. H. Spurgeon sermon series.
BV213.S65   1996   248.3'2—dc20   95-24910
                                                        CIP

ISBN 0-8254-3691-5 (pbk.)

        1 2 3 4 5 printing / year 00 99 98 97 96

Contents

1. The Mediation of Moses (Ex. 32:14) 5

2. Achsah's Asking: A Pattern of Prayer (Judg. 1:12–15) 15

3. The Prayer of Jabez (1 Chron. 4:10) 25

4. The Two Guards: Praying and Watching (Neh. 4:9) 38

5. The Young Man's Prayer (Ps. 90:14) 48

6. The Student's Prayer (Ps. 119:27) 61

7. Jesus Interceding for Transgressors (Isa. 53:12) 75

8. Daniel: A Pattern for Pleaders (Dan. 9:19) 89

9. "Lead Us Not into Temptation" (Matt. 6:13) 101

10. Peter's Shortest Prayer (Matt. 14:30) 115

11. The Preparatory Prayers of Christ (Luke 3:21–22;
    6:12–13; 9:28–29; Matt. 14:23–25; John 11:41–42;
    Luke 22:31–32; 23:46) 125

12. The Redeemer's Prayer (John 17:24) 136

13. John's First Doxology (Rev. 1:5–6) 147

3

1

The Mediation of Moses

And the LORD *repented of the evil which he thought to do unto his people (Exodus 32:14).*

I suppose that I need not say that this verse speaks after the manner of men. I do not know after what other manner we can speak. To speak of God after the manner of God is reserved for God Himself and mortal men could not comprehend such speech. In this sense the Lord often speaks, not according to literal fact, but according to the appearance of things to us, in order that we may understand so far as the human can comprehend the divine. The Lord's purposes never really change. His eternal will must forever be the same, for He cannot alter, since He would either have to alter for the better or for the worse. He cannot change for the better, for He is infinitely good; it were blasphemous to suppose that He could change for the worse. He who sees all things at once, and perceives at one glance the beginning and the end of all things, has no need to repent. "God is not a man, that he should lie; neither the son of man, that he should repent." But, in the course of His action, there appears to us to be sometimes a great change, and as we say of the sun that it rises and sets, though it does not actually do so, and we do not deceive when we speak after that fashion, so we say concerning God, in the language of the text, "The LORD repented of the evil which he thought to do unto his people." It appears to us to be so, and it is so in the act of God; yet this statement casts no doubt upon the great and glorious doctrine of the immutability of God.

Speaking after the manner of men, the mediation of Moses wrought this change in the mind of God. God in Moses seemed to overcome God out of Moses. God in the Mediator, the Man Christ Jesus, appears to be stronger for mercy than God apart from the Mediator. This saying of our

---

This sermon was taken from *The Metropolitan Tabernacle Pulpit* and was preached on Thursday evening, February 17, 1887.

5

text is very wonderful, and it deserves our most earnest and careful consideration.

Just think, for a minute, of Moses up there in the serene solitude with God. He had left the tents of Israel down below, and he had passed within the mystic circle of fire where none may come but he who is specially invited, and there, alone with God, Moses had a glorious season of fellowship with the Most High. He lent his listening ear to the instructions of the Almighty concerning the priesthood, and the tabernacle, and the altar; he was enjoying a profound peace of mind, when, on a sudden, he was startled. The whole tone of the speech of the Lord seemed changed, and He said to Moses, "Go, get thee down; for thy people, which thou broughtest out of the land of Egypt, have corrupted themselves." I can hardly imagine what thoughts passed through the great leader's mind. How Moses must have trembled in the presence of God! All the joy that he had experienced seemed suddenly to vanish, leaving behind, however, somewhat of the strength that always comes out of fellowship with God. This Moses now needed if ever he needed it in all his life, for this was the crucial period in the history of Moses, this was his severest trial, when, alone with God on the mountain's brow, he was called to come out of the happy serenity of his spirit, and to hear the voice of an angry God, saying, "Let me alone, that my wrath may wax hot against them, and that I may consume them."

The language of God was very stern, and well it might be after all that He had done for that people. When the song of Miriam had scarcely ceased, when you might almost hear the echoes of that jubilant note, "I will sing unto the Lord, for he hath triumphed gloriously: the horse and his rider hath he thrown into the sea," you might quickly have heard a very different cry, "Up, make us gods." In the presence of the calf that Aaron made, the same people blasphemously exclaimed, "These be thy gods, O Israel, which brought thee up out of the land of Egypt." Such a prostitution of their tongues to horrid blasphemies against Jehovah, such a turning aside from the truth to the grossest of falsehoods might well provoke the anger of a righteously jealous God.

It is noteworthy that Moses did not lose himself in this moment of trial. We read at once, "And Moses besought Jehovah the Lord his God." He was undoubtedly a man of prayer, but he must have been continually in the spirit of prayer, or else I could conceive of him, at that moment, falling on his face, and lying there in silent horror. I could imagine him flying down the mountain in a passionate haste to see what the people had done. It is delightful to find that he did neither of these two things, but that he began to pray. Oh, friends, if we habitually pray, we shall know how to pray when praying times become more pressing than usual! The man who is to wrestle with the angel must have been familiar with angels beforehand. You cannot go into your chamber and shut to the door and begin a mighty intercessory prayer if you have never been to the mercy seat before. No, Moses is "the man of God." You remember that he left us a prayer, in the Ninetieth Psalm, bearing this title, "A prayer of Moses the man of God." There is no man of God if there is no prayer, for prayer makes the man into the man of God. So, instinctively, though startled and saddened to the last degree, Moses is on his knees, beseeching the Lord his God.

Nothing Can Hinder a Truly Loving Spirit from Pleading for the Objects of Its Love

There were many things that might have hindered Moses from making intercessory prayer, and the first was *the startling greatness of the people's sin*. God Himself put it to Moses in strong language. He said, "Thy people . . . have corrupted themselves: they have turned aside quickly out of the way which I commanded them: they have made them a molten calf, and have worshiped it, and have sacrificed thereunto, and said, These be thy gods, O Israel, which have brought thee up out of the land of Egypt." This terrible accusation from the mouth of God, spoken as God would speak it, must have impressed Moses greatly with the awful character of Israel's sin, for farther on we find Moses saying to God, "Oh, this people have sinned a great sin, and have made them gods of gold." It has happened to you, I suppose, as it has to me, that in the sight of a great sin one has almost hesitated to pray about it. The person sinned so wantonly, under circumstances so peculiarly grievous, transgressed so willfully and so altogether without excuse, that you felt thrust back from the mercy seat and from pleading for such a sinner, but it was not so with Moses. Idolatry is a horrible sin, yet Moses is not kept back from pleading for its forgiveness. It astounds him, his own wrath waxes hot against it, but still, there he is, pleading for the transgressors. What else can he do but pray? And he does that after the best possible fashion. Oh, let us never say, when we see great sin, "I am appalled by it; I cannot pray about it; I am sickened by it, I loathe it." Some time ago, we had revelations of the most infamous criminality in this great city, which we cannot even now quite forget; I must confess that I sometimes felt as if I could not pray for some of the wretches who sinned so foully. But we must shake off that kind of feeling, and, even in the presence of the most atrocious iniquity, we must still say, "I will pray even for these Jerusalem sinners, that God may deliver them from the bondage of their sin."

A second thing that might have hindered Moses was not only the sin, but *the manifest obstinacy of those who had committed the sin*. Moses had it upon the evidence of the heart-searching God that these people were exceedingly perverse. The Lord said, "I have seen this people, and, behold, it is a stiffnecked people." Poor Moses had to learn, in after years, how true that saying was, for though he poured out his very soul for them and was tender toward them as a nurse with a child, yet they often vexed and wearied his spirit so that he cried to the Lord, "Have I conceived all this people? have I begotten them, that thou shouldest say unto me, Carry them in thy bosom, as a nursing father beareth the sucking child, unto the land which thou swarest unto their fathers?" He was crushed beneath the burden of Israel's perversity, yet, though God Himself had told him that they were a stiff-necked people, Moses besought the Lord concerning these obstinate sinners.

Then, thirdly, the prayer of Moses might have been hindered by *the greatness of God's wrath*, yet he said, "Lord, why doth thy wrath wax hot against thy people?" Shall I pray for the man with whom God is angry? Shall I dare to be an intercessor with God who is righteously wrathful? Why, some of us scarcely pray to the merciful God in this Gospel dispensation in which He is so full of goodness and long-suffering; there are some who profess to be God's people who make but very little intercession for the ungodly. I am afraid that, if they had seen God angry, they would have said, "It is of no use to pray for those idolaters. God is not unjustly angry. He knows what he does, and I must leave the matter there." But mighty love dares to cast itself upon its face before even an angry God; it dares to plead with Him and to ask Him, "Why doth thy wrath wax hot?" although it knows the reason and lays no blame upon the justice of God. Yes, love and faith together bring such a holy daring into the hearts of men of God that they can go into the presence of the King of Kings and cast themselves down before Him, even when He is in His wrath, and say, "O God, spare thy people; have mercy upon those with whom thou art justly angry"!

Perhaps it is an even more remarkable thing that Moses was not hindered from praying to God though to a large degree at the time, and much more afterward, *he sympathized with God in His wrath*. We have read how Moses' anger waxed hot when he saw the calf and the dancing; do you not see the holy man dashing the precious tablets upon the earth, regarding them as too sacred for the unholy eyes of idolaters to gaze upon? He saves them, as it were, from the desecration of contact with such a guilty people by breaking them to shivers upon the ground. Can you not see how his eyes flash fire as he tears down their idol, burns it in the fire, grinds it to powder, straws it upon the water, and makes them drink it? He is determined that it shall go into their very bowels; they shall be made to know what kind of a thing it was that they called a god. He was exceedingly wroth with Aaron; when he bade the sons of Levi draw the sword of vengeance and slay the audacious rebels, his wrath was fiercely hot, and rightly so. Yet he prays for the guilty people. Oh, never let your indignation against sin prevent your prayers for sinners! If the tempest comes on and your eyes flash lightnings and your lips speak thunderbolts, yet let the silver drops of pitying tears fall down your cheek and pray the Lord that the blessed shower may be acceptable to Him, especially when you plead for Jesus' sake. Nothing can stay the true lover of men's souls from pleading for them; no, not even our burning indignation against infamous iniquity. We see it and our whole blood boils at the sight, yet we betake ourselves to our knees and cry, "God be merciful to these great sinners and pardon them, for Jesus' sake!"

A still greater hindrance to the prayer of Moses than those I have mentioned was *God's request for the pleading to cease.* The Lord Himself said to the intercessor, "Let me alone." Oh, friends, I fear that you and I would have thought that it was time to leave off praying when the Lord with whom we were pleading said, "Let me alone, let me alone." But I believe that Moses prayed the more earnestly because of that apparent rebuff. Under the cover of that expression, if you look closely into it, you will see that Moses' prayer was really prevailing with God. Even before he had uttered it, while it was only being formed in his soul, Jehovah felt the force of it else He would not have said, "Let me alone."

And Moses appeared to gain courage from that which might have checked a less earnest suppliant; he seemed to say to himself, "Evidently God feels the force of my strong desires, and I will therefore wrestle with Him until I prevail." It was a real rebuff and was doubtless intended by the Lord to be the test of the patience, the perseverance, the confidence, the self-denying love of Moses. Jehovah says, "Let me alone, that my wrath may wax hot against them, and that I may consume them"; but Moses will not let Him alone. O you who love the Lord, give Him no rest until He saves men; though He Himself should seem to say to you, "Let me alone," do not let Him alone, for He wishes you to be importunate with Him, like that widow was with the unjust judge! The wicked man granted the poor woman's request because of her continual coming, and God is testing and trying you to see whether you really mean your prayers. He will keep you waiting a while and even seem to repulse you that you may, with an undaunted courage, say, "I will approach You; I will break through all obstacles to get to You. Even if it be not according to the law, I will go in to the King of Kings, and if I perish, I perish, but I will pray for sinners even if I perish in the act."

And, dear friends, there is one thing more that might have hindered the prayer of Moses. I want to bring this all out that you may see how tenderhearted love will pray in spite of every difficulty. *Moses prayed against his own personal interests*, for Jehovah said to him, Let me alone, that I may consume them," and then, looking with a glance of wondrous satisfaction upon His faithful servant, He said, "I will make of

thee a great nation." What an opportunity for an ambitious man! Moses
may become the founder of a great nation if he will. You know how men
and women, in those old days, panted to be the progenitors of innumerable peoples and looked upon it as the highest honor of mortal men that
their seed should fill the earth. Here is the opportunity for Moses to become the father of a nation that God will bless. All the benedictions of
Abraham, and Isaac, and Jacob, are to be met in Moses and his seed; but
no, he will not have it so. He turns to God and cries to Him still to bless
the sinful people. It seems as if he passed over the offer that God made,
sub silentio, as we say; leaving it in utter silence, he cries, "Spare thy
people, and bless thine heritage."

Nothing Can Deprive a Loving Spirit
of Its Arguments in Prayer for Others

It is one thing to be willing to besiege the throne of grace; it is quite
another thing to get the ammunition of prayer. Sometimes you cannot
pray, for prayer means the pleading of arguments, and there are times
when arguments fail you, when you cannot think of any reason why you
should pray. Now there was no argument in these people, nothing that
Moses could see in them that he could plead with God for them, so he
turned his eyes another way, he looked to God, and pleaded what he saw
in Him.

His first argument was that *the Lord had made them His people*. He
said, "LORD, why doth thy wrath wax hot against thy people?" The Lord
had said to Moses, "Get thee down; for thy people have corrupted themselves." "No," says Moses, "they are not *my* people; they are *Your* people." It was a noble "retort courteous," as it were, upon the ever-blessed
One. "In Your wrath You call them my people, but You know that they
are not mine; they are Yours. You chose their fathers and You entered
into covenant with them, and I remind You that they are Your chosen
ones, the objects of Your love and mercy; and therefore, O Lord, because
they are Yours, will You not bless them?" Oh, use that argument in your
supplications! If you cannot say of a sinner that he is God's chosen, at
least you can say that he is God's creature; therefore use that plea, "O
God, suffer not Your creature to perish!"

Next, Moses pleads that *the Lord had done great things for them*, for
he says, "Why doth thy wrath wax hot against thy people, which thou
hast brought forth out of the land of Egypt with great power, and with a
mighty hand?" "I never brought Israel out of Egypt," says Moses. "How
could I have done it? I did not divide the Red Sea; I did not smite
Pharaoh; You have done it, O Lord, You alone have done it. If You have
done all this, will You not finish what You have begun?" This was grand
pleading on the part of Moses, and I do not wonder that it prevailed.

Now, if you see any sign of grace, any token of God's work in the heart, plead it with the Lord. Say, "You have done so much, O Lord; be pleased to do the rest, and let these people be saved with Your everlasting salvation!"

Then Moses goes on to mention, in the next place, that *the Lord's name would be compromised if Israel should be destroyed*. He says, "Wherefore should the Egyptians speak, and say, For mischief did he bring them out, to slay them in the mountains, and to consume them from the face of the earth?" If God's people are not saved, if Christ does not see of the travail of His soul, the majesty of God and the honor of the Redeemer will be compromised. Shall Christ die to no purpose? Shall the Gospel be preached in vain? Shall the Holy Spirit be poured out without avail? Let us plead thus with God, and we shall not be short of arguments that we may urge with Him.

Moses goes on to mention that *God was in covenant with these people*. See how he puts it in the thirteenth verse: "Remember Abraham, Isaac, and Israel, thy servants, to whom thou swarest by thine own self, and saidst unto them, I will multiply your seed as the stars of heaven, and all this land that I have spoken of will I give unto your seed, and they shall inherit it forever." There is no pleading with God like reminding Him of His covenant. Get a hold of a promise of God, and you may pray with great boldness, for the Lord will not run back from His own word; but get a hold of the covenant, and you may plead with the greatest possible confidence. If I may compare a single promise to one great gun in the heavenly siege train, then the covenant may be likened to a whole park of artillery; with that, you may besiege heaven and come off a conqueror. Moses pleads thus with the Lord: "How can You destroy these people, even though You are angry with them, and they deserve Your wrath? You have promised to Abraham and Isaac and Jacob that their seed shall inherit the land, and if they be destroyed, how can they enter into Canaan and possess it?" This is grand pleading, but what bravery it was when Moses dared to say to God, "Remember thy covenant, and turn from thy fierce anger, and repent of thy thoughts of evil against thy people"! O Lord, teach us also how to plead like this!

Nor was Moses without another argument, the most wonderful of all. If you read in the next chapter, at the sixteenth verse, you will notice how Moses says to God, in effect, "*I cannot be parted from these people*; with them I will live; with them I will die. If You blot their name out of Your book, blot out my name also. If Your presence go not with me, carry us not up hence. For wherein shall it be known here that I and Your people have found grace in Your sight? is it not in that You go with us?" See how he puts it: "*I and thy people . . . thou goest with us.*" "No," says Moses, "I will not be favored alone; I will sink or swim with these people." And I do think that this is how the Lord Jesus Christ pleads for His church when He is interceding with God. "My Father," says He, I must have My people. My church is My bride, and I, the Bridegroom, cannot lose My spouse. I will die for her; if I live, she must live also; if I rise to glory, she must be brought to glory with Me." You see it is, "I and thy people"; this is the glorious conjunction of Christ with us as it was of Moses with the children of Israel. We never prevail in prayer so much as when we seem to link ourselves with the people for whom we pray. You cannot stand up above them as though you were their superior and then pray for them with any success; you must get down by the side of the sinner and say, "Let *us* plead with God." Sometimes when you are preaching to people or when you are praying for them, you must feel as if you could die for them, if they might be saved, and if they were lost it would seem as if you, too, had lost everything. Rutherford said that he should have two heavens if but one soul from Anwoth met him at God's right hand; doubtless, we shall have the same, and we have sometimes felt as if we had a hell at the thought of any of our hearers being cast into hell. When you can pray like that, when you put yourself side by side with the soul for which you are pleading, you will succeed. You will be like Elisha when he stretched himself upon the Shunammite's son, and put his mouth upon the child's mouth, his eyes upon the child's eye's, his hands upon the child's hands and seemed to identify himself with the dead child. Then was he made the means of quickening to the lad. God help us to plead thus in our prayers for sinners!

There is one other thing that I think has hardly ever been noticed and that is the way in which Moses finished his prayer by pleading *the sovereign mercy of the Lord*. When you are pleading with a man it is sometimes a very wise thing to stop your own pleading and let the man himself speak, and then out of his own mouth get your argument. When Moses pleaded with God for the people, he had at first only had an answer, and he turned around to the Lord and said, "You have favored me and promised to me great things; now I ask something more of You. I beseech You, show me Your glory." I do not think that was idle curiosity on the part of Moses, but that he meant to use it as the great master plea in prayer. When the Lord said to him, "I will make all my goodness pass before thee," I think I see the tears in the eyes of Moses, and I seem to hear him say, "He cannot smite the people, He cannot destroy them. He is going to make all His goodness pass before me, and I know what that is, infinite love, infinite mercy, mercy that endures forever." And then, when the Lord said, "I will proclaim the name of the LORD before thee; and will be gracious to whom I will be gracious, and will shew mercy on whom I will shew mercy," how the heart of Moses must have leaped within him as he said, "There it is, that glorious truth of divine sovereignty; the Lord will show mercy on whom He will show mercy. Why, then, He can have mercy on these wicked wretches who have been making a god out of a calf and bowing before it!" I do delight, sometimes, to fall back upon the sovereignty of God and say, "Lord, here is a wicked wretch; I cannot see any reason why You should save him! I can see many reasons why You should damn him; but then You do as You will. Oh, magnify Your sovereign grace by saving this great sinner! Let men see what a mighty King You are, and how royally You handle the silver scepter of Your pardoning mercy."

That is a grand argument, for it gives God all the glory; it puts Him upon the throne; it acknowledges that He is an absolute Sovereign who is not to be dictated to or held in with bonds and cords. Shall He not do as He wills with His own? We need often to listen to the sublime truth that thunders out from the throne of God, "I will have mercy on whom I will have mercy, and I will have compassion on whom I will have compassion. So then it is not of him that willeth, nor of him that runneth, but of God that showeth mercy." Out of this truth comes the best plea that ever trembles on a pleader's lips. "Great King, eternal, immortal, invisible, have mercy upon us! Divine Sovereign, exercise Your gracious dispensing power, and let the guilty rebels live!"

Nothing Can Hinder a Pleading Spirit of Success

If you and I know how to plead for sinners, there is no reason why we should not succeed, for, first, there is no reason *in the character of God.* Try, if you can, to get some idea of what God is, and though you tremble before His sovereignty and adore His holiness and magnify His justice, remember that He is still, first and foremost, love. "God is love," and that love shines in all the divine attributes. It is undiminished in its glory by any one of them. All the attributes of God are harmonious with each other, and love seems to be the very center of the circle. Let us never be afraid of pleading with God. He will never take it ill on our part that we pray for sinners, for it is so much after his own mind. "As I live, saith the Lord GOD, I have no pleasure in the death of the wicked; but that the wicked turn from his way and live." The character of God is infinitely gracious; even in its sovereignty, it is grace that reigns; therefore, let us never be afraid of pleading with the Lord. We shall surely succeed, for there is nothing in God's character to hinder us.

And, next, there is nothing *in God's thought* to hinder the pleader's success. Look at the text: "The Lord repented of the evil which he thought to do unto his people." I will therefore never be hindered in my pleading by any idea of the divine purpose, whatever that purpose may be. There are some who have dreaded what they call "the horrible decrees of God." No divine decree is horrible to me and it shall never hinder me in pleading with the Lord for the salvation of men. He is God; therefore let Him do what seems Him good, absolute authority is safe enough in His hands. But even if He had thought to do evil to His people, there is no reason why we should cease from praying; we may yet succeed, for so the text has it, "Jehovah repented of the evil which he thought to do unto his people."

I will go yet farther and say that there is nothing even *in God's act* to hinder us from pleading with success. If God has begun to smite the sinner, as long as that sinner is in this world, I will still pray for him. Remember, how, when the fiery rain was falling upon Sodom and Gomorrah, and the vile cities of the plain were being covered with its bituminous sleet, Zoar was preserved in answer to the prayers of Lot. Look at David; he was a great sinner, and he had brought upon his people a terrible plague, and the destroying angel stood with his drawn sword stretched out over Jerusalem; but when David saw the angel, he said to the Lord, "Lo, I have sinned, and I have done wickedly: but these sheep, what have they done?" So the Lord was entreated for the land, and the plague was stayed from Israel. Why, if I saw you between the very jaws of hell, so long as they had not actually engulfed you, I would pray for you! God forbid that we should sin against any guilty ones by ceasing to pray for them however desperate their case! My text seems to me to put this matter with astonishing force and power; the evil which God had thought to do was prevented by the intercession of His servant Moses.

The Mediation of Christ Is Greater Than That of Moses

Nothing in the mediation of Moses can match our greater intercessor, the Lord Jesus Christ. Remember, brethren, that He not only prayed and willingly offered Himself to die for us, but *He actually died for us*. His name was blotted from the book of the living, He died that we might live. He went not to God saying, "Peradventure, I may make atonement for the guilty"; but *He made the atonement, and His pleading for sinners is perpetually prevalent*. God is hearing Christ at this moment as He makes intercession for the transgressors, and He is giving Him to see of the travail of His soul. This being the case, nothing ought to prevent any sinner from pleading for himself through Jesus Christ. If you think that God means to destroy you, yet go and pray to Him, for "The Lord repented of the evil which he thought to do unto his people." Thus may He deal in mercy with you, for His dear Son's sake! Amen.

2
Achsah's Asking: A Pattern of Prayer

And Caleb said, He that smiteth Kirjath-sepher, and taketh it, to him will I give Achsah my daughter to wife. And Othniel the son of Kenaz, Caleb's younger brother, took it: and he gave him Achsah his daughter to wife. And it came to pass, when she came to him, that she moved him to ask of her father a field: and she lighted from off her ass; and Caleb said unto her, What wilt thou? And she said unto him, Give me a blessing: for thou hast given me a south land; give me also springs of water. And Caleb gave her the upper springs and the nether springs (Judges 1:12–15).

In domestic life we often meet with pictures of life in the house of God. I am sure that we are allowed to find them there, for our Savior said, "If ye then, being evil, know how to give good gifts unto your children: how much more shall your heavenly Father give the Holy Spirit to them that ask him?" God is a Father, and He likens Himself to us as fathers; we who are believers are God's children, and we are permitted to liken ourselves to our own children. Just as our children would deal with us and we would deal with them, so may we deal with God and expect God to deal with us. This little story of a daughter and her father is recorded twice in the Bible. You will find it in the fifteenth chapter of the book of Joshua, as well as in this first chapter of the book of Judges. It is not inserted twice without good reasons. I am going to use it tonight simply in this manner—the way in which this woman went to her father and the way in which her father treated her may teach us how to go to our Father who is in heaven, and what to expect if we go to Him in that fashion.

This sermon was taken from *The Metropolitan Tabernacle Pulpit* and was preached on Sunday evening, June 2, 1889.

I would hold up this good woman, Achsah, before you tonight as a kind of model, or parable. Our parable shall be Achsah, the daughter of Caleb; she shall be the picture of the true successful pleader with our Father in heaven.

Her Consideration of the Matter

Achsah was newly married, and she had an estate to go with her to her husband. She naturally wished that her husband should find in that estate all that was convenient and all that might be profitable; looking it all over, *she saw what she wanted.* Before you pray, know what you are needing. That man who blunders down on his knees with nothing in his mind will blunder up again and get nothing for his pains. When this young woman goes to her father to ask for something, she knows what she is going to ask. She will not open her mouth until first her heart has been filled with knowledge as to what she requires. She saw that the land her father gave her would be of very little use to her husband and her because it wanted water springs. She therefore goes to her father with a very definite request, "Give me also springs of water."

My dear friends, do you always, before you pray, think of what you are going to ask? "Oh!" says somebody, "I utter some good words." Does God want your words? Think what you are going to ask before you begin to pray, and then pray like business men. This woman does not say to her father, "Father, listen to me," and then utter some pretty little oration about nothing; she knows what she is going to ask for and why she is going to ask it. She sees her need, and she prizes the boon she is about to request. Oh, take note, you who are much in prayer, that you rush not to the holy exercise "as the horse rushes into the battle"; that you venture not out upon the sea of prayer without knowing within a little whereabouts will be your port! I do believe that God will make you think of many more things while you are in prayer; the Spirit will help your infirmities and suggest to you other petitions, but before a word escapes your lips, I counsel you to do what Achsah did, know what you really need.

This good woman, before she went to her father with her petition, *asked her husband's help.* When she came to her husband, "she moved him to ask of her father a field." Now, Othniel was a very brave man, and very brave men are generally very bashful men. It is your cowardly man who is often forward and impertinent. But Othniel was so bashful that he did not like asking his uncle Caleb to give him anything more; it looked like grasping. He had received a wife from him, and he had received land from him, and he seemed to say, "No, my good wife, it is all very well for you to put me up to this, but I do not feel like asking for anything more for myself." Still, learn this lesson, good wives, prompt your husbands to pray with you. Brothers, ask your brothers to pray with you. Sisters, be not satisfied to approach the throne of grace alone, but ask your sister to pray with you. It is often a great help in prayer for two of you to agree touching the thing that concerns Christ's kingdom. A cordon of praying souls around the throne of grace will be sure to prevail. God help us to be anxious in prayer to get the help of others! A friend, some time ago, said to me, "My dear pastor, whenever I cannot pray for myself, and there are times when I feel shut up about myself, I always take to praying for you: 'God bless him, at any rate!' and I have not long been praying for you before I begin to feel able to pray for myself." I should like to come in for many of those odd bits of prayer. Whenever any of you get stuck in the mud, do pray for me. It will do you good, and I shall get a blessing. Remember how it is written of Job, "The Lord turned the captivity of Job, when he prayed for his friends." While he prayed for himself, he remained a captive, but when he prayed for those unfriendly friends of his, then the Lord smiled upon him and loosed his captivity. So it is a good thing in prayer to imitate this woman, Achsah. Know what you want, and then ask others to join with you in prayer. Wife, especially ask your husband; husband, especially ask your wife. I think there is no sweeter praying on earth than the praying of a husband and a wife together when they plead for their children and when they invoke a blessing upon each other and upon the work of the Lord.

Next, Achsah bethought herself of this one thing, that *she was going to present her request to her father*. I suppose that she would not have gone to ask of anybody else, but she said to herself, "Come, Achsah, Caleb is your father. The boon I am going to ask is not of a stranger who does not know me, but of a father, in whose care I have been ever since I was born." This thought ought to help us in prayer, and it will help us when we remember that we do not go to ask of an enemy nor to plead with a stranger, but we say, "Our Father, which art in heaven." Do you mean it? Do you really believe that God is your Father? Do you feel the spirit of sonship in your heart? If so, this ought to help you to pray with a believing tone. Your Father will give you whatever you need. If there was anything that I wanted and I should ask it of him, I expect that my dear father, old and feeble as he is, would give it to me if it were within the range of his possibility; surely, our great and glorious Father, with whom we have lived ever since we were newborn, has favored us so much that we ought to ask very boldly and with a childlike familiarity, resting assured that our Father will never be vexed with us because we ask these things. Indeed, He knows what things we have need of before we ask Him.

So this good woman, Achsah, feeling that it was her father of whom she was going to ask and seeing that her husband hesitated to join her in her request, made the best of her way to go and pray alone. "Well, well, Othniel, I would have liked you to have gone with me, but as you will not, I am going alone." So she gets upon the ass, which was a familiar way for ladies to ride in that day, and she rides off to her father. The grand old man sees his daughter coming, and by the very look of her he knows that she is coming on business; there is a something about her eye that tells him she is coming with a request. This was not the first time that she had asked something of him. He knew her usual look when she was about to petition him, so he goes to meet her, and she alights from her ass, a token of great and deep respect, just as Rebecca, when she saw Isaac, alighted from the camel. She wished to show how deeply she reverenced that grand man, of whom it was an honor to be a child. Caleb survived Joshua a little while and still in his old age went out to fight the Canaanites and conquered Hebron, which the Lord had given him. Achsah pays reverence to her father, but yet she is very hearty in what she is going to say to him.

Now, dear friends, learn again from this good woman how to pray. *She went humbly, yet eagerly.* If others will not pray with you, go alone; when you go, go very reverently. It is a shameful thing that there should ever be an irreverent prayer. You are on earth, and God is in heaven; multiply not your words as though you were talking to your equal. Do not speak to God as though you could order Him about and have your will of Him, and He were to be a lackey to you. Bow low before the Most High; own yourself unworthy to approach Him, speaking in the tone of one who is pleading for that which must be a gift of great charity. So shall you draw near to God aright; but while you are humble, have desire in your eyes and expectation in your countenance. Pray as one who means to have what he asks. Say not, as one did, "I ask once for what I want; and if I do not get it, I never ask again." That is unchristian. Plead on if you know that what you are asking is right. Be like the importunate widow; come again and again and again. Be like the prophet's servant, "Go again seven times." You will at last prevail. This good woman had not to use importunity. The very look of her showed that she wanted something; therefore her father said, "What wilt thou?"

I think that, at the outset of our meditation, we have learned something that ought to help us in prayer. If you put even this into practice, though no more was said, you might go away blessed thereby. God grant us to know our need, to be anxious to have the help of our fellow believers, but to remember that, as we go to our Father, even if nobody will go with us, we may go alone through Jesus Christ our Lord and plead our case with our Father in heaven!

Her Encouragement

"Oh!" says one, "I could ask anything if my father said to me, 'What wilt thou?'" This is precisely what your great Father does say to you tonight, "What wilt thou?" With all the magnanimity of His great heart, God manifests Himself to the praying man or pleading woman, and He says, "What wilt thou? What is thy petition, and what is thy request?"

What do I gather from that question, "What wilt thou?" Why, this. First, *you should know what you want.* Could some Christians here, if God were to say to each of them, "What wilt thou?" answer Him? Do you not think that we get into such an indistinct, indiscriminate kind of a way of praying that we do not quite know what we do really want? If it is so with you, do not expect to be heard until you know what you want. Get a distinct, definite request realized by your mind as a pressing want; get it right before your mind's eye as a thing that you must have. That is a blessed preparation for prayer. Caleb said to his daughter, "What wilt thou?" and Christ says to you tonight, "Dear child of Mine, what do you want of Me? Blood-bought daughter, what do You want of Me?" Will you not, some of you, begin to find a request or two if you have not one ready on the tip of your tongue? I hope that you have many petitions lying in the center of your hearts and that they will not be long in leaping to your lips.

Next, as you ought to know what you want, *you are to ask for it.* God's way of giving is through our asking. I suppose that He does that in order that He may give twice over, for a prayer is itself a blessing as well as the answer to prayer. Perhaps it sometimes does us as much good to pray for a blessing as to get the blessing. At any rate, this is God's way, "Ask, and ye shall receive." He puts even His own Son, our blessed Savior, under this rule, for He says even to Him, "Ask of me, and I shall give thee the heathen for thine inheritance, and the uttermost parts of the earth for thy possession." It is a rule, then, without exception, that you are to know what you want, and you are to ask for it. Will you do this, dear friend, while the Lord says to you, "What wilt thou?"

And when Caleb said, "What wilt thou?" did he not as good as say to Achsah, *"You shall have what you ask for"*? Come, now, tonight is a sweet, fair night for praying; I do not know a night when it is not so, but tonight is a delightful night for prayer. You shall have what you ask. "All things, whatsoever ye shall ask in prayer, believing, ye shall receive." Desires written in your heart by the Holy Spirit will all of them be fulfilled. Come, then, bethink you of these three things: you must know what you want, you must ask for what you want, and you shall have what you want. Your Father says to you, as Caleb said to Achsah, "What wilt thou?"

And, once more, *it shall be a pleasure to your Father to hear you ask.* There stands Caleb, that good, brave, grand man, and he says to his daughter, "What wilt thou?" He likes to see her open that mouth that is so dear to him; he loves to listen to the music of her voice. The father delights to hear his child tell him what she wants, and it shall be no displeasure to your God to hear you pray tonight. It shall be a joy to Him to have your petition spread before Him. Many fathers would quite as soon that their children did not tell them all their wants; in fact, the fewer their wants, the better pleased will their parents are. But our Father in heaven feels a pleasure in giving to us all we need, for giving does not impoverish Him and withholding would not enrich Him. He as much delights to give as the sun delights to shine. It is the very element of God to be scattering bounties. Come, then, and pray to Him; you will thus please Him more than you will please yourself. I wish that I could so speak tonight that every child of God here would say, "The preacher is talking to me. He means that I have to pray and that God will hear me and bless me." Yes, that is precisely what I do mean. Take my advice, and prove it yourself tonight; see if it is not so, that God takes delight in your poor, feeble, broken prayer and grants your humble petition.

Thus we have seen Achsah's consideration before prayer and her encouragement to pray.

Her Prayer

As soon as she found that she had an audience with her father of the kindliest sort, she said to him, "*Give me a blessing.*" I like that petition; it is a good beginning, "Give me a blessing." I should like to put that prayer into every believing mouth here tonight, "Give me a blessing. Whatever You do not give me, give me a blessing. Whatever else You give me, do not fail to give me a blessing." A father's blessing is an inheritance to a loving child. "Give me a blessing." What is the blessing of God? If He shall say, "Thou art blessed," you may defy the Devil to make you cursed. If the Lord calls you blessed, you are blessed. Though covered with boils, as Job was, you are blessed. Though near to death, like Lazarus, with the dogs licking his sores, you are blessed. If you should be dying, like Stephen, beneath the stones of murderous enemies, if God bless you, what more can you wish for? No, Lord, put me anywhere that you will, as long as I get your blessing. Deny me what You will, only give me Your blessing. I am rich in poverty, if You do bless me. So Achsah said to her father, "Give me a blessing." I wish that prayer might be prayed by everybody here tonight. Printers here tonight, pray for once, if you have not prayed before, "Lord, give me a blessing." Soldiers, pray your gracious God to give you a blessing. Young men and maidens, old men and fathers, take this prayer of Achsah's upon your hearts tonight, "Give me a blessing." Why, if the Lord shall hear that prayer from everybody in this place, what a blessed company we shall be; we shall go our way to be a blessing to this city of London beyond what we have ever been before!

Notice next, in Achsah's prayer, how *she mingled gratitude with her petition*: "Give me a blessing: for thou hast given me a south land." We like, when people ask anything of us, to hear them say, "You did help me, you know, sir, a month ago"; but if they seem to come to you and quite forget that you ever helped them and never thank you, never say a word about it, but come begging again and again, you say to yourself, "Why, I helped that fellow a month ago! He never says a word about that." "Have I not seen you before?" "No, sir; I do not know that you ever have." "Ah!" you say to yourself, "he will get no more out of me. He is not grateful for what he has had." I do believe that ingratitude seals up the springs of blessing. When we do not praise God for what we have received from Him, it seems to me but just that He should say, "I am not going to cast my pearls before swine. I shall not give my precious things to those who set no value upon them." When you are praying, take to praising also; you will gather strength thereby. When a man has to take a long jump, you have seen him go back a good distance and then run forward to get a spring. Go back in grateful praise to God for what He has done for you in days gone by, and then get a spring for your leap for a future blessing or a present blessing. Mingle gratitude with all your prayers.

There was not only gratitude in this woman's prayer, but *she used former gifts as a plea for more*: "Thou hast given me a south land; give me also." Oh, yes, that is grand argument with God: "You have given me; therefore, give me some more." You cannot always use this argument with men, for if you remind them that they have given you so much, they say, "Well, now, I think that somebody else must have a turn. Could you not go next door?" It is never so with God. There is no argument with Him like this, "Lord, You have done this to me; You are always the same; your all-sufficiency is not abated; therefore, do again what You have done!" Make every gift that God gives you a plea for another gift; when you have that other gift, make it a plea for another gift. He loves you to do this. Every blessing given contains the eggs of other blessings within it. You must take the blessing and find the hidden eggs and let them be hatched by your earnestness, and there shall be a whole brood of blessings springing out of a single blessing. See you to that.

But this good woman *used this plea in a particular way*: she said, "Thou hast given me a south land; give me also springs of water." This was as much as to say, "Though you have given me the south land, and I thank you for it, it is no good to me unless I have water for it. It is a very hot bit of ground, this south land; it wants irrigating. My husband and I

cannot get a living from it unless you give us springs of water." Do you
see the way you are to pray? "Lord, You have given me so much, and it
will all be good for nothing if You do not give me more. If You do not
finish, it is a pity that You ever began; You have given me very many
mercies, but if I do not have many more, all your generosity will be lost.
You do not begin to build unless You mean to finish and so I come to
You to say, You have given me a south land, but it is dry; give me also
springs of water to make it of real value to me." In this prayer of
Achsah's there is a particularity and a speciality: "Give me also springs
of water." She knew what she was praying for; that is the way to pray.
When you ask of God, ask distinctly: "Give me springs of water." You
may say, "Give me my daily bread." You may cry, "Give me a sense of
pardoned sin." You may distinctly ask for anything that God has
promised to give, but mind that, like this woman, you are distinct and
plain in what you ask of God: "Give me springs of water."

Now, it seems to me, tonight, as if I could pray that prayer, "Give me
springs of water." "Lord, You have given me a south land, all this congregation, Sunday after Sunday, all this multitude of people; but, Lord, how
can I preach to them if You do not give me springs of water? All my fresh
springs are in You. What is the use of the hearers if there is not the power
of the Holy Spirit going with the Word to bless them? Give me springs of
water." Now, I can suppose a Sunday school teacher here tonight saying,
"Lord, I thank You for my interesting class and for the attention that the
scholars pay to what I say to them, but, Lord, what is the good of my
children to me unless You give me springs of water? Oh, that, out of myself, out of my very soul, I might have the power of Your Holy Spirit with
all my teaching! Give me springs of water." I can imagine a Christian
parent here saying, "Lord, I thank You for my wife and my children; I
thank You for all these, but what is the use of my being the head of a family unless You give me springs of grace that, like David, I may bless my
household and see my children grow up in Your fear? Give me springs of
water." The point of this petition is this, "O Lord, what You have given
me is of little good to me unless You give me something more." O dear
hearers, if God has given you money, pray that He will give you grace to
use it aright, or else, if you hoard it up or spend it, it may, in either case,
prove a curse to you! Pray, "Give me springs of water; give me grace to
use my wealth aright." Some here have many talents. Riches in the brain
are among the best of riches. Be thankful to God for your talents, but cry,
"Lord, give me of Your grace, that I may use my talents for Your glory.
Give me springs of water, or else my talents shall be a dry and thirsty
land, yielding no fruit to You. Give me springs of water." You see, the
prayer is not merely for water, but for springs of water. "Give me a perpetual, eternal, ever-flowing fountain. Give me grace that shall never fail

but shall flow and flow on and flow forever. Give me a constant supply: Give me springs of water."

This woman's prayer, then, I have thus tried to commend to you. Oh, that we might all have grace to copy her!

Her Success

Observe, *her father gave her what she asked.* She asked for springs, and he gave her springs. "If a son shall ask bread of any of you that is a father, will he give him a stone? Or if he ask a fish, will he for a fish give him a serpent?" God gives us what we ask for when it is wise to do so. Sometimes we make mistakes and ask for the wrong thing, and then He is kind enough to put the pen through the petition and write another word into the prayer and answer the amended prayer rather than the first foolish edition of it. Caleb gave Achsah what she asked.

Next, *he gave her in large measure.* She asked for springs of water, and he gave her the upper springs and the nether springs. The Lord "is able to do exceeding abundantly above all that we ask or think." Some use that passage in prayer and misquote it, "above what we can ask or even think." That is not in the Bible; you can ask or even think anything you like; it is "above all that we ask or think." Our asking or our thinking falls short, but God's giving never does.

And *her father gave her this without a word of upbraiding.* He did not say, "Ah, you Achsah, you are always begging of me!" He did not say, "Now that I have given you to your husband, it is too bad of him to let you come and ask for more from me when I have given you plenty already." There are some gruff old fathers who would speak like that to their daughters and say, "No, no, no! Come, come, I cannot stand this; you have a good portion already, my girl, and I have others to think of as well as you." No, Caleb gave her the upper and the nether springs and never said a word by way of blaming her, but I will be bound to say that he smiled on her as he said, "Take the upper and the nether springs, and may you and your husband enjoy the whole! You have only asked, after all, what my heart delights to give you." Now, may the Lord grant to us tonight to ask of Him in wisdom, and may He not have to upbraid us, but give us all manner of blessings both of the upper and the nether springs, both of heaven and earth, both of eternity and time, and give them freely, and not say even a single word by way of upbraiding us!

I have done with this last point when I have asked a plain question or two. Why is it that, tonight, some of you dear friends have a very parched-up inheritance? The grass will not grow, and the corn will not grow; nothing good seems to grow. You have been plowing and turning the plot up and sowing and weeding and yet nothing comes of it. You are a believer, and you have an inheritance, but you are not very much given to song, not very cheery, not very happy, and you are sitting here tonight and singing to the tune Job—

> Lord, what a wretched land is this,
>   That yields us no supply!

Well, why is that? There is no need for it. Your heavenly Father does not want you to be in that miserable condition. There is something to be had that would lift you out of that state and change your tone altogether. May every child of God here go to his Father, just like Achsah went to Caleb! Pour out your heart before the Lord with all the simple ease and naturalness of a trustful, loving child.

Do you say, "Oh, I could not do that"? Then I shall have to ask you this question, Are we truly the children of God if we never feel toward Him any of that holy boldness? Do you not think that every child must feel a measure of that confidence toward his father? If there is a son in the world who says, "No, I–I–I really could not speak to my father," well, I shall not make any inquiries, but I know that there is something wrong at his home; there is something not right either with the father or with the boy. Wherever there is a loving home, you never hear the son or daughter say, "You know, I–I–I could not ask my father." I hope that we have none of us gotten into that condition with regard to our earthly fathers; let none of us be in that condition with regard to our heavenly Father.

> My soul, ask what thou wilt,
>   Thou canst not be too bold;
> Since his own blood for thee he spilt
>   What else can he withhold?

Come, then, while in the pew tonight, before we gather at the communion table, and present your petition with a childlike confidence, and expect it to be heard, and expect tonight to have fellowship with the Father and with His Son Jesus Christ.

And you, poor sinners, who cannot pray like children, what are you to do? Well, you remember how the Savior said to the Syrophenician woman, "It is not meet to take the children's bread, and to cast it unto the dogs." But she answered, "Yes, Lord: yet the dogs under the table eat of the children's crumbs." You come in for the crumbs tonight; for if a man is satisfied to eat crumbs with the dogs, God will not be satisfied until He makes him eat bread with the children. If you will take the lowest place, God will give you a higher place before long. Come to Jesus, and trust in Him henceforth and forever. Amen.

3

The Prayer of Jabez

Oh that thou wouldest bless me indeed (1 Chronicles 4:10).

We know very little about Jabez except that he was more honorable than his brethren and that he was called Jabez because his mother bare him with sorrow. It will sometimes happen that where there is the most sorrow in the antecedents, there will be the most pleasure in the sequel. As the furious storm gives place to the clear sunshine, so the night of weeping precedes the morning of joy. Sorrow is the harbinger; gladness is the prince it ushers in. Cowper says:

> The path of sorrow, and that path alone,
> Leads to the place where sorrow is unknown.

To a great extent we find that we must sow in tears before we can reap in joy. Many of our works for Christ have cost us tears. Difficulties and disappointments have wrung our souls with anguish. Yet those projects that have cost us more than ordinary sorrow have often turned out to be the most honorable of our undertakings. While our grief called the offspring of desire *Benoni*, "the son of my sorrow," our faith has been afterward able to give it a name of delight, *Benjamin*, "the son of my right hand." You may expect a blessing in serving God if you are enabled to persevere under many discouragements. The ship is often long coming home because detained on the way by excess of cargo. Expect her freight to be the better when she reaches the port. More honorable than his brethren was the child whom his mother bore with sorrow. As for this Jabez, whose aim was so well pointed, his fame so far sounded, his name so lastingly embalmed—he was a man of prayer. The honor he enjoyed would not have been worth having if it had not been vigorously contested and equitably won. His devotion was the key to his promotion.

This sermon was taken from *The Metropolitan Tabernacle Pulpit* and was preached at the Metropolitan Tabernacle, Newington, in 1871.

Those are the best honors that come from God, the award of grace with the acknowledgment of service. When Jacob was surnamed Israel, he received his princedom after a memorable night of prayer. Surely it was far more honorable to him than if it had been bestowed upon him as a flattering distinction by some earthly emperor. The best honor is that which a man gains in communion with the Most High. Jabez, we are told, was more honorable than his brethren, and his prayer is forthwith recorded, as if to intimate that he was also more prayerful than his brethren. We are told of what petitions his prayer consisted. All through it is very significant and instructive. We have only time to take one clause of it—indeed, that one clause may be said to comprehend the rest: "Oh that thou wouldest bless me indeed!" I commend it as a prayer for ourselves, dear brethren and sisters; one that will be available at all seasons, a prayer to begin Christian life with, a prayer to end it with, a prayer that would never be unseasonable in your joys or in your sorrows.

Oh, that You, the God of Israel, the covenant God, would bless me indeed! The very pith of the prayer seems to lie in that word "indeed." There are many varieties of blessing. Some are blessings only in name; they gratify our wishes for a moment but permanently disappoint our expectations. They charm the eye but pall on the taste. Others are mere temporary blessings; they perish with the using. Though for awhile they regale the senses, they cannot satisfy the higher cravings of the soul. But, "Oh that thou wouldest bless me indeed!" I know whom God blesses shall be blessed. The thing good in itself is bestowed with the goodwill of the giver and shall be productive of so much good fortune to the recipient that it may well be esteemed as a blessing "indeed," for there is nothing comparable to it. Let the grace of God prompt it, let the choice of God appoint it, let the bounty of God confer it, and then the endowment shall be something godlike indeed, something worthy of the lips that pronounce the benediction, and verily to be craved by every one who seeks honor that is substantial and enduring. "Oh that thou wouldest bless me indeed!" Think it over, and you will see that there is a depth of meaning in the expression.

We may set this in contrast with human blessings: "Oh that thou wouldest bless me indeed!" It is very delightful to be blessed by our parents and those venerable friends whose benedictions come from their hearts and are backed up by their prayers. Many a poor man has had no other legacy to leave his children except his blessing, but the blessing of an honest, holy, Christian father is a rich treasure to his children. One might well feel it were a thing to be deplored through life if he had lost a parent's blessing. We like to have it. The blessing of our spiritual parents is consolatory. Though we believe in no priestcraft, we like to live in the affections of those who were the means of bringing us to Christ and from whose lips we were instructed in the things of God. And how very precious is the blessing of the poor! I do not wonder that Job treasured that up as a sweet thing. "When the ear heard me, then it blessed me." If you have relieved the widow and the fatherless, and their thanks are returned to you in benediction, it is no mean reward. But, dear friends, after all—all that parents, relatives, saints, and grateful persons can do in the way of blessing falls very far short of what we desire to have. O Lord, we would have the blessings of our fellow creatures, the blessings that come from their hearts, but, "Oh that *thou* wouldest bless me indeed!" for You can bless with authority. Their blessings may be but words, but Yours are effectual. They may often wish what they cannot do and desire to give what they have not at their own disposal, but Your will is omnipotent. You created the world with but a word. O that such omnipotence would now bespeak me Your blessing! Other blessings may bring us some tiny cheer, but in Your favor is life. Other blessings are mere tittles in comparison with Your blessing, for Your blessing is the title "to an inheritance incorruptible" and unfading, to "a kingdom which cannot be moved."

Well therefore might David pray in another place, "With thy blessing let the house of thy servant be blessed for ever." Perhaps in this place, Jabez may have put the blessing of God in contrast with the blessings of men. Men will bless you when you do well for yourself. They will praise the man who is successful in business. Nothing succeeds like success. Nothing has so much the approval of the general public as a man's prosperity. Alas! they do not weigh men's actions in the balances of the sanctuary but in quite other scales. You will find those about you who will commend you if you are prosperous, or like Job's comforters, condemn you if you suffer adversity. Perhaps there may be some feature about their blessings that may please you because you feel you deserve them. They commend you for your patriotism; you have been a patriot. They commend you for your generosity; you know you have been self-sacrificing. Well, but after all, what is there in the verdict of man? At a trial, the verdict of the policeman who stands in the court, or of the spectators who sit in the courthouse, amounts to just nothing. The man who is being tried feels that the only thing that is of importance at all will be the verdict of the jury and the sentence of the judge. So it will little avail us, whatever we may do, how others commend or censure. Their blessings are not of any great value. But, "Oh that thou wouldest bless me," that You would say, "Well done, good and faithful servant." Commend You the feeble service that through Your grace my heart has rendered. That will be to bless me indeed.

Men are sometimes blessed in a very fulsome sense by flattery. There are always those who, like the fox in the fable, hope to gain the cheese by praising the crow. They never saw such plumage, and no voice could be so sweet as yours. The whole of their mind is set not on you, but on what they are to gain by you. The race of flatterers is never extinct, though the flattered usually flatter themselves it is so. They may conceive that men flatter others, but all is so palpable and transparent when heaped upon themselves that they accept it with a great deal of self-complacency, as being perhaps a little exaggerated, but after all exceedingly near the truth. We are not very apt to take a large discount off the praises that others offer us; yet, were we wise, we should press to our bosom those who censure us, and we should always keep at arm's length those who praise us, for those who censure us to our face cannot possibly be making a market of us. But with regard to those who extol us, rising early and using loud sentences of praise, we may suspect, and we shall very seldom be unjust in the suspicion, that there is some other motive in the praise which they render to us than that which appears on the surface.

Young man, are you placed in a position where God honors you? Beware of flatterers. Or have you come into a large estate? Have you abundance? There are always flies where there is honey. Beware of flattery. Young woman, are you fair to look upon? There will be those about you that will have their designs, perhaps their evil designs, in lauding your beauty. Beware of flatterers. Turn aside from all these who have honey on their tongues, because of the poison of asps that is under it. Bethink you of Solomon's caution, "Meddle not with him that flattereth with his lips." Cry to God, "Deliver me from all this vain adulation which nauseates my soul." So shall you pray to Him the more fervently, "Oh that thou wouldest bless me indeed!" Let me have Your benediction which never says more than it means, which never gives less than it promises. If you take then the prayer of Jabez as being put in contrast with the benedictions that come from men, you see much force in it.

But we may put it in another light and compare the blessing Jabez craved with those blessings that are temporal and transient. There are many bounties given to us mercifully by God for which we are bound to be very grateful, but we must not set too much store by them. We may accept them with gratitude, but we must not make them our idols. When we have them we have great need to cry, "Oh, that You would bless me indeed and make these inferior blessings real blessings." If we have them not, we should with greater vehemence cry, "Oh, that we may be rich in faith, and if not blessed with these external favors, may we be blessed spiritually, and then we shall be blessed indeed."

Let us review some of these mercies and just say a word or two about them.

One of the first cravings of men's hearts is wealth. So universal the desire to gain it that we might almost say it is a natural instinct. How many have thought if they once possessed it, they should be blessed indeed! But there are ten thousand proofs that happiness consists not in the abundance that a man possesses. So many instances are well known to you all that I need not quote any to show that riches are not a blessing indeed. They are rather apparently than really so. Hence, it has been well said that when we see how much a man has we envy him, but could we see how little he enjoys we should pity him. Some that have had the most easy circumstances have had the most uneasy minds. Those who have acquired all they could wish, had their wishes been at all sane, have been led by the possession of what they had to be discontented because they had not more.

> Thus the base miser starves amidst his store,
> Broods o'er his gold, and griping still at more,
> Sits sadly pining, and believes he's poor.

Nothing is more clear to anyone who chooses to observe it than that riches are not the chief good at whose advent sorrow flies and in whose presence joy perennial springs. Full often wealth cozens the owner. Dainties are spread on his table, but his appetite foils; minstrels wait his bidding, but his ears are deaf to all the strains of music; holidays he may have as many as he pleases, but for him recreation has lost all its charms. Or he is young, fortune has come to him by inheritance, and he makes pleasure his pursuit until sport becomes more irksome than work, and dissipation worse than drudgery. You know how riches make themselves wings; like the bird that roosted on the tree they fly away. In sickness and despondency these ample means that once seemed to whisper, "Soul, take your ease," prove themselves to be poor comforters. In death they even tend to make the pang of separation more acute because there is the more to leave, the more to lose. We may well say, if we have wealth, "My God, put me not off with these husks; let me never make a god of the silver and the gold, the goods and the chattels, the estates and investments, which in Your providence You have given me. I beseech You, bless me indeed. As for these worldly possessions, they will be my bane unless I have Your grace with them." And if you have not wealth, and perhaps the most of you will never have it, say, "My Father, You have denied me this outward and seeming good, enrich me with Your love, give me the gold of Your favor, bless me indeed, then allot to others whatever You will, You shall divide my portion, my soul shall wait Your daily will; do bless me indeed, and I shall be content."

Another transient blessing that our poor humanity fondly covets and eagerly pursues is fame. In this respect we would fain be more honorable than our brethren and outstrip all our competitors. It seems natural to us all to wish to make a name and gain some note, in the circle we move in, at any rate, and we wish to make that circle wider if we can. But here, as of riches, it is indisputable that the greatest fame does not bring with it any equal measure of gratification. Men, in seeking after notoriety or honor, have a degree of pleasure in the search that they do not always possess when they have gained their object. Some of the most famous men have also been the most wretched of the human race. If you have honor and fame, accept it, but let this prayer go up, "My God, bless me indeed, for what profit were it, if my name were in a thousand mouths, if You should spew it out of Your mouth? What matter though my name were written on marble, if it were not written in the Lamb's Book of Life? These blessings are only apparently blessings, windy blessings, blessings that mock me. Give me Your blessing, then the honor which comes of You will make me blessed indeed." If you happen to have lived in obscurity, and have never entered the lists for honors among your fellowmen, be content to run well your own course and fulfill truly your own vocation. To lack fame is not the most grievous of ills; it is worse to have it like the snow that whitens the ground in the morning and disappears in the heat of the day. What matters it to a dead man that men are talking of him? Get the blessing indeed.

There is another temporal blessing that wise men desire and legitimately may wish for rather than the other two—*the blessing of health.* Can we ever prize it sufficiently? To trifle with such a boon is the madness of folly. The highest eulogiums that can be passed on health would not be extravagant. He that has a healthy body is infinitely more blessed than he who is sickly, whatever his estates may be. Yet if I have health, my bones well set and my muscles well strung, if I scarcely know an ache or pain but can rise in the morning and with elastic step go forth to labor and cast myself upon my couch at night and sleep the sleep of the happy, yet, oh, let me not glory in my strength! In a moment it may fail me. A few short weeks may reduce the strong man to a skeleton. Consumption may set in; the cheek may pale with the shadow of death. Let not the strong man glory in his strength. The Lord "delighteth not in the strength of the horse: he taketh not pleasure in the legs of a man." And let us not make our boast concerning these things. Say, you that are in good health, "My God, bless me indeed. Give me the healthy soul. Heal me of my spiritual diseases. *Jehovah Rophi,* come and purge out the leprosy that is in my heart by nature. Make me healthy in the heavenly sense that I may not be put aside among the unclean, but allowed to stand among the congregation of Your saints. Bless my bodily health to me that I may use it rightly, spending the strength I have in

Your service and to Your glory; otherwise, though blessed with health, I may not be blessed indeed."

Some of you, dear friends, do not possess the great treasure of health. Wearisome days and nights are appointed you. Your bones are become an almanac in which you note the changes of the weather. There is much about you that is fitted to excite pity. But I pray that you may have the blessing indeed, and I know what that is. I can heartily sympathize with a sister that said to me the other day, "I had such nearness to God when I was sick, such full assurance, and such joy in the Lord. I regret to say I have lost it now, that I could almost wish to be ill again, if thereby I might have a renewal of communion with God." I have oftentimes looked gratefully back to my sick chamber. I am certain that I never did grow in grace one half so much anywhere as I have upon the bed of pain. It ought not to be so. Our joyous mercies ought to be great fertilizers to our spirits, but not infrequently our griefs are more salutary than our joys. The pruning knife is best for some of us. Well, after all, whatever you have to suffer, of weakness, of debility, of pain, and of anguish, may it be so attended with the divine presence that this light affliction may work out for you a far more exceeding and eternal weight of glory, and so you may be blessed indeed.

I will only dwell upon one more temporal mercy which is very precious—I mean *the blessing of home*. I do not think anyone can ever prize it too highly or speak too well of it. What a blessing it is to have the fireside and the dear relationships that gather around the word *home*—wife, children, father, brother, sister! Why, there are no songs in any language that are more full of music than those dedicated to Mother. We hear a great deal about the German Fatherland—we like the sound. But the word *Father* is the whole of it. The *land* is nothing; the *Father* is key to the music. There are many of us, I hope, blessed with a great many of these relationships. Do not let us be content to solace our souls with ties that must before long be sundered. Let us ask that over and above them may come the blessing indeed. I thank You, my God, for my earthly father, but oh, be You my Father, then am I blessed indeed. I thank You, my God, for a mother's love, but comfort You my soul as one whom a mother comforts, then am I blessed indeed. I thank You, Savior, for the marriage bond, but be You the bridegroom of my soul. I thank You for the tie of brotherhood, but be You my brother born for adversity, bone of my bone, and flesh of my flesh.

The home You have given me I prize, and thank You for it; but I would dwell in the house of the Lord forever and be a child that never wanders, wherever my feet may travel, from my Father's house with its many mansions. You can thus be blessed indeed. If not domiciled under the paternal care of the Almighty, even the blessing of home, with all its sweet familiar comforts, does not reach to the benediction which Jabez desired for himself. But do I speak to any here that are separated from kith and kin? I know some of you have left behind you in the bivouac of life graves where parts of your heart are buried, and that which remains is bleeding with just so many wounds. Ah, well the Lord bless you indeed! Widow, your Maker is your husband. Fatherless one, He has said, "I will not leave you comfortless: I will come to you." Oh, to find all your relationships made up in Him, then you will be blessed indeed! I have perhaps taken too long a time in mentioning these temporary blessings, so let me set the text in another light. I trust we have had human blessings and temporary blessings to fill our hearts with gladness, but not to foul our hearts with worldliness or to distract our attention from the things that belong to our everlasting welfare.

Let us proceed, thirdly, to speak of *imaginary blessings*. There are such in the world. From them may God deliver us. "Oh that thou wouldest bless me indeed!" Take the Pharisee. He stood in the Lord's house, and he thought he had the Lord's blessing, and it made him very bold, and he spoke with unctuous self-complacency, "God, I thank thee, that I am not as other men are," and so on. He had the blessing, and well indeed he supposed himself to have merited it. He had fasted twice in the week, paid tithes of all that he possessed, even to the odd farthing on the mint and the extra halfpenny on the cummin he had used. He felt he had done everything. His the blessing of a quiet or a quiescent conscience; good, easy man. He was a pattern to the parish. It was a pity everybody did not live as he did; if they had, they would not have wanted any police. Pilate might have dismissed his guards, and Herod his soldiers. He was just one of the most excellent persons that ever breathed. He adored the city of which he was a burgess! Aye; but he was not blessed indeed. This was in his own overweening conceit. He was a mere wind-bag, nothing more, and the blessing that he fancied had fallen upon him had never come. The poor publican whom he thought accursed went to his home justified rather than he. The blessing had not fallen on the man who thought he had it. Oh, let every one of us here feel the sting of this rebuke and pray, "Great God, save us from imputing to ourselves a righteousness which we do not possess. Save us from wrapping ourselves up in our own rags and fancying we have put on the wedding garments. Bless me indeed. Let me have the true righteousness. Let me have the true worthiness You can accept, even that which is of faith in Jesus Christ."

Another form of this imaginary blessing is found in persons who would scorn to be thought self-righteous. Their delusion, however, is near akin. I hear them singing—

> I do believe, I will believe,
> That Jesus died for me;
> And on his cross he shed his blood,
> From sin to set me free.

You believe it, you say. Well, but how do you know? Upon what authority do you make so sure? Who told you? "Oh, I believe it." Yes, but we must mind what we believe. Have you any clear evidence of a special interest in the blood of Jesus? Can you give any spiritual reasons for believing that Christ has set you free from sin? I am afraid that some have got a hope that has not gotten any ground, like an anchor without any fluke—nothing to grasp, nothing to lay hold upon. They say they are saved, and they stick to it. They are and think it wicked to doubt it, yet they have no reason to warrant their confidence. When the sons of Kohath carried the ark and touched it with their hands, they did rightly; when Uzzah touched it, he died. There are those who are ready to be fully assured; there are others to whom it will be death to talk of it. There is a great difference between presumption and full assurance. Full assurance is reasonable; it is based on solid ground. Presumption takes for granted and with brazen face pronounces that to be its own to which it has no right whatever. Beware, I pray you, of presuming that you are saved. If with your heart you do trust in Jesus, then are you saved, but if you merely say, "I trust in Jesus," it does not save you. If your heart be renewed, if you shall hate the things that you did once love and love the things that you did once hate, if you have really repented, if there be a thorough change of mind in you, if you be born again, then have you reason to rejoice. But if there be no vital change, no inward godliness; if there be no love to God, no prayer, no work of the Holy Spirit, then your saying, "I am saved," is but your own assertion, and it may delude, but it will not deliver you. Our prayer ought to be, "Oh that you would bless me indeed, with real faith, with real salvation, with the trust in Jesus that is the essential of faith, not with the conceit that begets credulity. God preserve us from imaginary blessings!" I have met with persons who said, "I believe I am saved because I dreamed it," or, "Because I had a text of Scripture that applied to my own case." "Such and such a good man said so and so in his sermon," or, "Because I took to weeping and was excited, and felt as I never felt before." Ah! but nothing will stand the trial but this, "Do you abjure all confidence in everything but the finished work of Jesus, and do you come to Christ to be reconciled in Him to God?" If you do not, your dreams and visions and fancies are but dreams and visions and fancies and will not serve your turn when most you need them. Pray the Lord to bless you indeed, for of that sterling verity in all your walk and talk there is a great scarcity.

Too much, I am afraid, even those who are saved—saved for time and eternity—need this caution and have good cause to pray this prayer, that they may learn to make a distinction between some things that they think to be spiritual blessings and others that are blessings indeed. Let me show you what I mean. Is it certainly a blessing to get an answer to your prayer after your own mind? I always like to qualify my most earnest prayer with, "Not as I will, but as You will." Not only ought I to do it, but I would like to do it, because otherwise I might ask for something that it would be dangerous for me to receive. God might give it me in anger, and I might find little sweetness in the grant but much soreness in the grief it caused me. You remember how Israel of old asked for flesh, and God gave them quails, but while the meat was yet in their mouths, the wrath of God came upon them. Ask for the meat, if you like, but always put in this: "Lord, if this is not a real blessing, do not give it me." "Bless me indeed."

I hardly like to repeat the old story of the good woman whose son was ill—a little child near death's door—and she begged the minister, a Puritan, to pray for his life. He did pray very earnestly, but he put in, "If it be Your will, save this child." The woman said, "I cannot hear that. I must have you pray that the child shall live. Do not put in any *ifs* or *buts*." "Woman," said the minister, "it may be you will live to rue the day that ever you wished to set your will up against God's will." Twenty years afterward, she was carried away in a fainting fit from under Tyburn gallows-tree, where that son was put to death as a felon. Although she had lived to see her child grow up to be a man, it would have been infinitely better for her had the child died and infinitely wiser had she left it to God's will. Do not be quite so sure that what you think an answer to prayer is any proof of divine love. It may leave much room for you to seek to the Lord, saying, "Oh that thou wouldest bless me indeed!" So sometimes great exhilaration of spirit, liveliness of heart, even though it be religious joy, may not always be blessing. We delight in it, and oh, sometimes when we have had gatherings for prayer here, the fire has burned, and our souls have glowed! We felt at the time how we could sing—

> My willing soul would stay
> In such a frame as this,
> And sit and sing herself away
> To everlasting bliss.

So far as that was a blessing we are thankful for it, but I should not like to set such seasons up as if my enjoyments were the main token of God's favor or as if they were the chief signs of His blessing. Perhaps it would be a greater blessing to me to be broken in spirit and laid low before the Lord at the present time. When you ask for the highest joy and pray to be on the mountain with Christ, remember it may be as much a blessing, yes, a blessing indeed, to be brought into the Valley of Humiliation, to be laid very low and constrained to cry out in anguish, "Lord, save, or I perish!"

> If today he deigns to bless us
> With a sense of pardon'd sin,
> He tomorrow may distress us,
> Make us feel the plague within,
> All to make us
> Sick of self, and fond of him.

These variable experiences of ours may be blessings indeed to us when, had we been always rejoicing, we might have been like Moab, settled on our lees and not emptied from vessel to vessel. It fares ill with those who have no changes; they fear not God. Have we not, dear friends, sometimes envied those persons that are always calm and unruffled and are never perturbed in mind? Well, there are Christians whose evenness of temper deserves to be emulated. And as for that calm repose, that unwavering assurance that comes from the spirit of God, it is a very delightful attainment, but I am not sure that we ought to envy anybody's lot because it is more tranquil or less exposed to storm and tempest than our own. There is a danger of saying, "Peace, peace," where there is no peace, and there is a calmness that arises from callousness. Dupes there are who deceive their own souls. They have no doubts, they say, but it is because they have little heart searching. They have no anxieties, because they have not much enterprise or many pursuits to stir them up. Or it may be they have no pains because they have no life. Better go to heaven halt and maimed than go marching on in confidence down to hell. "Oh that thou wouldest bless me indeed!" My God, I will envy no one his gifts or his graces, much less his inward mood or his outward circumstances, if only You will "bless me indeed." I would not be comforted unless You comfort me, nor have any peace but Christ my peace, nor any rest but the rest that comes from the sweet savor of the sacrifice of Christ. Christ shall be all in all, and none shall be anything to me save Him. O that we might always feel that we are not to judge as to the manner of the blessing but must leave it with God to give us what we would have, not the imaginary blessing, the superficial and apparent blessing, but the blessing indeed!

Equally too with regard to our work and service, I think our prayer should always be, "Oh that thou wouldest bless me indeed!" It is lamentable to see the work of some good men, though it is not ours to judge them, how very pretentious, how very unreal it is. It is really shocking to think how some men pretend to build up a church in the course of two or three evenings. They will report, in the corner of the newspapers, that there were forty-three persons convinced of sin and forty-six justified and, sometimes, thirty-eight sanctified; I do not know what besides of wonderful statistics they give as to all that is accomplished. I have observed congregations that have been speedily gathered together, and great additions have been made to the church all of a sudden. And what has become of them? Where are those churches at the present moment? The dreariest deserts in Christendom are those places that were fertilized by the patent manures of certain revivalists. The whole church seemed to have spent its strength in one rush and effort after something, and it ended in nothing at all. They built their wooden house and piled up the hay and made a stubble spire that seemed to reach the heavens, and there fell one spark, and all went away in smoke, and he that came to labor next time—the successor of the great builder—had to get the ashes swept away before he could do any good. The prayer of every one that serves God should be, "Oh that thou wouldest bless me indeed." Plod on, plod on. If I only build one piece of masonry in my life and nothing more, if it be gold, silver, or precious stones, it is a good deal for a man to do; of such precious stuff as that, to build even one little corner that will not show is a worthy service. It will not be much talked of, but it will last. There is the point: it will last. "Establish thou the work of our hands upon us; yea, the work of our hands establish thou it." If we are not builders in an established church, it is of little use to try at all. What God establishes will stand, but what men build without His establishment will certainly come to nothing. "Oh that thou wouldest bless me indeed!" Sunday school teacher, be this your prayer. Tract distributor, local preacher, whatever you may be, dear brother or sister, whatever your form of service, do ask the Lord that you may not be one of those plaster builders using sham compo that only requires a certain amount of frost and weather to make it crumble to pieces. Be it yours, if you cannot build a cathedral, to build at least one part of the marvelous temple that God is building for eternity, which will outlast the stars.

I have one thing more to mention before I bring this sermon to a close. *The blessings of God's grace are blessings indeed*, which in right earnest we ought to seek after. By these marks shall you know them. Blessings indeed are such blessings as come from the pierced hand; blessings that come from Calvary's bloody tree, streaming from the Savior's wounded side—your pardon, your acceptance, your spiritual life, the bread that is meat indeed, the blood that is drink indeed, your oneness to Christ and all that comes of it—these are blessings indeed. Any blessing that comes as the result of the Spirit's work in your soul is a blessing indeed; though it humble you, though it strip you, though it kill you, it is a blessing indeed. Though the harrow go over and over your soul, and the deep plow cut into your very heart; though you be maimed and wounded and left for dead, yet if the Spirit of God do it, it is a blessing indeed. If He convinces you of sin, of righteousness, and of judgment, even though you have not hitherto been brought to Christ, it is a blessing indeed. Anything that He does, accept it; do not be dubious of it, but pray that He may continue His blessed operations in your soul. Whatsoever leads you to God is in like manner a blessing indeed. Riches may not do it. There may be a golden wall between you and God. Health will not do it; even the strength and marrow of your bones may keep you at a distance from your God. But anything that draws you nearer to Him is a blessing indeed. What though it be a cross that raises you? Yet if it raise you to God, it shall be a blessing indeed. Anything that reaches into eternity with a preparation for the world to come, anything that we can carry across the river—the holy joy that is to blossom in those fields beyond the swelling flood, the pure cloudless love of the brotherhood which is to be the atmosphere of truth forever—anything of this kind that has the eternal broad arrow on it—the immutable mark—is a blessing indeed. And anything that helps me to glorify God is a blessing indeed. If I be sick, and that helps me to praise Him, it is a blessing indeed. If I be poor, and I can serve Him better in poverty than in wealth, it is a blessing indeed. If I be in contempt, I will rejoice in that day and leap for joy, if it be for Christ's sake—it is a blessing indeed. Yes, my faith shakes off the disguise, snatches the vizor from the fair forehead of the blessing, and counts it all joy to all into divers trials for the sake of Jesus and the recompense of reward that He has promised. "Oh that we may be blessed indeed!"

Now, I send you away with these three words. *Search.* See whether the blessings are blessings indeed, and be not satisfied unless you know that they are of God, tokens of His grace, and earnests of His saving purpose. *Weigh*—that shall be the next word. Whatever you have, weigh it in the scale, and ascertain if it be a blessing indeed, conferring such grace upon you as causes you to abound in love and to abound in every good word and work. And lastly, *Pray.* So pray that this prayer may mingle with all your prayers, that whatsoever God grants or whatever He withholds you may be blessed indeed. Is it a joy time with you? O that Christ may mellow your joy and prevent the intoxication of earthly blessedness from leading you aside from close walking with Him! In the night of sorrow, pray that He will bless you indeed, lest the wormwood also intoxicate you and make you drunk, lest your afflictions should make you think hardly of Him. Pray for the blessing, which having, you are rich to all the intents of bliss, or which lacking, you are poor and destitute though plenty fill your store. "If thy presence go not with me, carry us not up hence." But "Oh that thou wouldest bless me indeed!"

4

The Two Guards: Praying and Watching

Nevertheless we made our prayer unto our God, and set a watch against them day and night, because of them (Nehemiah 4:9).

Nehemiah and the Jews with him were rebuilding the walls of Jerusalem. Sanballat and others were angry with them and tried to stop the work. They determined to pounce upon the people on a sudden and slay them and so to put an end to what they were doing. Our text tells us what Nehemiah and his companions did in this emergency: "Nevertheless we made our prayer unto our God, and set a watch against them day and night, because of them."

These people had not only to build the wall of Jerusalem but to watch against their enemies at the same time. Their case is ours. We have to work for Christ. I hope that all of us who love Him are trying to do what we can to build up His kingdom. But we need also to watch against deadly foes. If they can destroy us, of course they will also destroy our work. They will do both if they can. The powers of evil are mad against the people of God. If they can in any way injure or annoy us, you may rest assured that they will do so. They will leave no stone unturned, if it can serve their purpose. No arrows will be left in the quivers of hell while there are godly men and women at whom they can be aimed. Satan and his allies will aim at our hearts every poisoned dart they have.

Nehemiah had been warned of the attack that was to be made upon the city. The Jews who lived near these Samaritans had heard their talk of what they meant to do, and they came and told Nehemiah of the plotting of the adversaries. We also have been warned. As our Lord said to Peter, "Simon, Simon, behold, Satan hath desired to have you, that he

---

This sermon was taken from *The Metropolitan Tabernacle Pulpit* and was preached on Thursday evening, July 24, 1890.

may sift you as wheat," so has He, in His Word, told us that there is a great and terrible evil power that is seeking our destruction. If Satan can do it, he will not only sift us as wheat, but he will cast us into the fire that we may be destroyed. Brethren, we are not ignorant of his devices. You are not left in a fool's paradise to dream of security from trial and to fancy that you are past temptation.

It was well for these people, also, that, being in danger and being aware of the malice of their enemies, they had a noble leader to incite them to the right course to be pursued. Nehemiah was well qualified for his work. He gave the Jews very shrewd, sensible, and yet spiritual advice, and this was a great help to them in their hour of need. Beloved, we have a better Leader than Nehemiah; we have our Lord Jesus Christ Himself, and we have His Holy Spirit who dwells in us and shall be with us. I beg you to listen to His wise and good advice. I think He will give it to you through our explanation of the text. He will say to you what Nehemiah, in effect, said to these people, "Watch and pray." Although the adversaries of the Jews conspired together and came to fight against Jerusalem and to hinder the work of rebuilding the wall, Nehemiah says, "Nevertheless we made our prayer unto our God, and set a watch against them day and night, because of them."

In the text, I see two guards; first, *prayer*: "We made our prayer unto our God." The second guard is *watchfulness*: "We . . . set a watch." When I have spoken on these two subjects, I shall take, as my third topic, *the two guards together*. "We prayed, . . . and set a watch." We must have them both if we would defeat the Enemy.

The First Guard: Prayer

Speaking of this prayer, I would hold it up as a pattern for our prayers in a like condition. It was *a prayer that meant business*. Sometimes when we pray I am afraid that we are not transacting business at the throne of grace, but Nehemiah was as practical in his prayer as he was in the setting of the watch. Some brethren get up in our prayer meetings and say some very good things, but what they really ask for I am sure I do not know. I have heard prayers of which I have said when they were over, "Well, if God answers that prayer, I have not the least idea what He will give us." It was a very beautiful prayer, and there was a great deal of explanation of doctrine and experience in it, but I do not think that God wants to have doctrine or experience explained to Him. The fault about the prayer was that there was not anything asked for in it. I like when brethren are praying that they should be as businesslike as a good carpenter at his work. It is of no use to have a hammer with an ivory handle unless you aim at the nail you mean to drive in up to the head; if that is your object, an ordinary hammer will do as well as a fine one, perhaps better. Now, the prayers of Nehemiah and the Jews were petitions for divine protection. They knew what they wanted, and they asked for it definitely. Oh, for more definiteness in prayer! I am afraid our prayers are often clouds, and we get mists for answers. Nehemiah's prayers meant business. I wish we could always pray in this way. When I pray, I like to go to God just as I go to a banker when I have a check to be cashed. I walk in, put the check down on the counter, the clerk gives me my money, I take it up and go about my business. I do not know that I ever stopped in a bank five minutes to talk with the clerks; when I have received my change, I go away and attend to other matters. That is how I like to pray. But there is a way of praying that seems like lounging near the mercy seat as though one had no particular reason for being found there. Let it not be so with you, brethren. Plead the promise, believe it, receive the blessing God is ready to give, and go about your business. The prayer of Nehemiah and his companions meant business.

In the next place, it was *a prayer that overcame difficulties*. The text begins with a long word, "nevertheless." If we pull it to pieces, we get three words, *never the less*; when certain things happen, we will pray never the less; on the contrary, we will cry to our God all the more. Sanballat sneered; we prayed never the less, but all the more because of his sneers. Tobiah uttered a cutting jest; we prayed never the less, but all the more because of his mocking taunt. If men make a jest of your religion, pray none the less. If they even become cruel and violent to you, pray none the less; never the less, not a word less, not a syllable less, not a desire less, and not any faith less. What are your difficulties, dear friend, in coming to the mercy seat? What hindrance lies in your way? Let nothing obstruct your approach to the throne of grace. Turn all stumbling stones into stepping-stones; come with holy boldness and say, notwithstanding all opposition, "never the less, we made our prayer unto our God." Nehemiah's prayer meant business and overcame difficulties.

Notice, next, that it was *a prayer that came before anything else*. It does not say that Nehemiah set a watch and then prayed but "nevertheless we made our prayer unto our God, and set a watch." Prayer must always be the forehorse of the team. Do whatever else is wise, but not until you have prayed. Send for the physician if you are sick, but first pray. Take the medicine if you have a belief that it will do you good, but first pray. Go and talk with the man who has slandered you, if you think you ought to do so, but first pray. "Well, I am going to do so and so," says one, "and I shall pray for a blessing on it afterward." Do not begin it until you have prayed. Begin, continue, and end everything with prayer, but especially begin with prayer. Some people would never begin what they are going to do if they prayed about it first, for they could not ask God's blessing upon it. Is there anybody here who is going out of this tabernacle to a place where he should not go? Will he pray first? He knows that he cannot ask a blessing on it; therefore he ought not to go there. Go nowhere where you cannot go after prayer. This would often be a good guide in your choice of where you should go. Nehemiah first prayed, and then set a watch.

Once more, it was *a prayer that was continued*. If I read the passage aright, "we made our prayer unto our God, and set a watch against them day and night," it means that, as long as they watched, they prayed. They did not pray their prayer and then leave off and go away, as naughty boys do when they give runaway knocks at a door. Having begun to pray, they continued praying. So long as there were any enemies about, the prayer and the watching were never parted. They continued still to cry to Him who keeps Israel as long as they set the watchman of the night to warn them of the foe.

When shall we leave off praying, brothers and sisters? Well, they say that we shall do so when we get to heaven. I am not clear about that. I do not believe in the intercession of saints for us, but I remember that it is written in the book of Revelation that the souls under the altar cried, "How long, O Lord?" Those souls are waiting for the resurrection, waiting for the coming of Christ, waiting for the triumph of His kingdom, and I cannot conceive of their waiting without often crying, "O Lord, how long? Remember Your Son, glorify His name, accomplish the number of Your elect." But certainly, as long as we are here we must pray. One lady, professed that she had long been perfect and that her mind was in such complete conformity with the mind of God that she need not pray any longer. Poor creature! What did she know about the matter? She needed to begin at the first letter of the alphabet of salvation and pray, "God be merciful to me, a sinner"! When people imagine they need not to pray, the Lord have mercy upon them!

> Long as they live let Christians pray,
> For only while they pray they live.

The prayer that Nehemiah offered was, next, *a prayer that was home-made*. There may be some of you who like prayers made for you; it may be that if all in the congregation are to join in the supplication and every voice is to speak, the prayer must be prepared even as the hymn is, but ready-made prayers always seem to me very much like ready-made clothes—they are meant to fit everybody, and it is very seldom that they fit anybody. For real business at the mercy seat, give me a homemade prayer, a prayer that comes out of the deeps of my heart, not because I invented it, but because God the Holy Spirit put it there and gave it such living force that I could not help letting it come out. Though your words are broken and your sentences disconnected, if your desires are earnest, if they are like coals of juniper burning with a vehement flame, God will not mind how they find expression. If you have no words, perhaps you will pray better without them than with them. There are prayers that break the backs of words; they are too heavy for any human language to carry.

This prayer, then, whatever it may have been as to its words, was one the pleaders made: "We made our prayer unto our God."

It is very important to notice, however, that it was *a prayer that went to the home of prayer:* "We made our prayer unto our God." You have heard of the man who prayed at Boston, "the hub of the universe," and the report in the paper the next morning was that "The Rev. Dr. So-and-so prayed the finest prayer that was ever addressed to a Boston audience." I am afraid that there are some prayers of that sort, that are prayed to the congregation. That is not the kind of prayer that God loves. Forget that there is anybody present, forget that a human ear is listening to your accents, and let it be said of your prayer, "Nevertheless we made our prayer unto our God."

It is a very commonplace remark to make that prayer must go to God if it is to be of any avail, but it is very necessary to make it. When prayer does not go to God, what is the good of it? When you come out of your closet and feel that you have only gone through a form, how much are you benefited? Make your prayer to your God. Speak in His ear knowing that He is there; come away knowing that He has replied to you, that He has lifted up the light of His countenance upon you. That is the kind of prayer we need for our protection against our enemies both day and night.

Only once more upon this first point. I gather from the words before me that it was *a prayer saturated with faith.* We made our prayer unto— God? No, "unto our God." They had taken Jehovah to be their God, and they prayed to Him as their God. They had a full assurance that, though He was the God of the whole earth, yet He was specially their God; so they made their prayer to the God who had given Himself to them and to whom they belonged by covenant relationship. "We made our prayer unto *our God.*" Those two little words carry a vast weight of meaning. The door of prayer seems to turn on those two golden hinges—"our God." If you and I are to be delivered from the evil that is in the world, if we are to be kept building the church of God, we must have for our first guard, mighty, believing prayer such as Nehemiah and his Jewish friends presented to the Lord.

The Second Guard: Watching

This setting of the watch was a work appointed. "We set a watch." Nehemiah did not say, "Now, some of you fellows, go and watch," leaving the post of watchman open to any who chose to take it, but they "set a watch." A certain number of men had to go on duty at a certain point, at a certain hour, and remain for a certain length of time, and to be on guard against the adversary. "We set a watch." Brethren, if we are to watch over ourselves, and we must do so, we must do it with a definite purpose. We must not say, "I must try to be watchful." No, no; you must be watchful; your watchfulness must be as distinct and definite an act as your prayer. "We set a watch." Some of you have seen the guards changed at the barracks; there is a special time for each company to mount guard. When you go to bed at night, pray the Lord to guard you during the darkness. In the morning, set a watch when you go to your business. Set a watch when you go to the dinner table; set a watch when you return home. Oh, how soon we may be betrayed into evil unless we set a watch!

It was *a work carefully done*, for Nehemiah says, "We set a watch against them day and night, because of them." These last three words would be better rendered, "ever against them"; that is, wherever there was an enemy, there he set a watch. They are likely to come up this way. Very well, set a watch there. Perhaps they may shift about and come up this way. Very well, set a watch there. Possibly they may come climbing over the wall in front here. Well, set a watch there. "We set a watch over against them." One brother has a very hot temper. Brother, set a watch there. Another is very much inclined to levity. Brother, set a watch there. Another is very morose at home, critical, picking holes in other people's coats. Brother, set a watch there. One friend has a tendency to pride, another to unbelief. Set a watch wherever the foe is likely to come. "We made our prayer unto our God, and set a watch over against them."

It was *a work continued;* Nehemiah says, "we set a watch against them day and night." What! is there to be somebody sitting up all night? Of course there is. If Sanballat had told them when he meant to attack them, they might have gone to sleep at other times; But as he did not give them that information, they had to set a watch "day and night." The Devil will not give you notice when he is going to tempt you; he likes to take men by surprise; therefore, set up watch day and night.

It was *a work quickened by knowledge*. They knew that Sanballat would come if he could, so they set a watch. The more you know of the plague of your own heart, the more you will set a watch against it. The more you know of the temptations that are in the world through lust, the more should you set a watch. The older you are, the more you should watch. "Oh!" says an aged friend, "you should not say that; it is the young people who go wrong." Is it? In the Old Testament or in the New, have you an instance of a young believer who went astray? The Bible tells us of many old men who were tripped up by Satan when they were not watching; so you have need to set a watch even when your hair turns gray, for you will not be out of gunshot of the Devil until you have passed through the gate of pearl into the golden streets of the New Jerusalem.

You and I, dear friends, have need to set a watch against the enemies of our holy faith. People ask me, "Why do you talk so much about the 'downgrade'? Let men believe what they like. Go on with your work for God and pray to Him to set them right." I believe in praying and setting a watch. We have to guard with jealous care "the faith once for all delivered to the saints." When you find, as you do find now, professing Christians and professing Christian ministers denying every article of the faith or putting another meaning upon all the words than they must have been understood to bear and preaching lies in the name of the Most High, it is time that somebody set a watch against them. A night watchman's place is not an easy berth, but I am willing to take that post for my blessed Master's sake. Those professed servants of Christ who enter into an unholy alliance with men who deny the faith will have to answer for it at the last great day. As for us, brethren, when our Lord comes, let Him find us watching as well as praying.

But, dear friends, to come home to ourselves, we must set a watch against our own personal adversaries. I hope that, in one sense, you have no personal enemies, that you owe nobody a grudge, but that you live in peace and love toward all mankind. But there are Christian people here who will go to homes where everybody in the house is against them. Many a godly woman goes from the sanctuary to a drunken husband; many children, converted to God, see anything but what they like to see in their homes. What are they to do in such circumstances? Set a watch. Dear woman, how do you know but that you shall be the means of saving your unconverted husband? If so, you must set a watch; do not give him a bit of your mind; you will not convert him that way. And you, dear children who have come to Christ and joined the church, mind that you are dutiful and obedient, for otherwise you will destroy all hope of bringing your parents to the Savior. Set a watch, set a watch. "Oh!" say you, "if I do a little wrong, they magnify it." I know they do; therefore, set a watch; be more careful. Set a watch over your temper, set a watch over your tongue, set a watch over your actions. Be patient, be gentle, be hoping. May the Spirit of God work all this in you!

But there is another set of enemies much more dreadful than these adversaries that are without us—the foes within, the evil tendencies of our corrupt nature, against which we must always set a watch. Perhaps you say, "How can I do this?" Well first know what they are. People who are beginning the Christian life should seek to know where their weak points are. I should not wonder, dear friend, if your weak point lies where you think that you are strong. Where you think, "Oh, I shall never go wrong there!"—that is the very place where you are likely to fall. Set a watch wherever any weakness has appeared, and if you have in the past of your Christian life grieved the Holy Spirit by anything wrong, set a double watch there. Where you tripped once, you may trip again, for you are the same man. Set a watch, also, dear friend, whenever you feel quite secure. Whenever you feel certain that you cannot be tempted in a particular direction, that proves that you are already as proud as Lucifer. Set a watch, set a watch, set a watch. Avoid every occasion of sin. If any course of conduct would lead you into sin, do not go in that direction. I heard a man say, as an excuse for drinking, "You see, if ever I take a glass of beer, I seem to lose myself, and I must have two or three more." Well, then, if that is the case with you, do not take a glass of beer. "But," says one, "if I get into company, I forget myself." Then, do not go into company. Better go to heaven as a hermit than go to hell with a multitude. Pluck out your right eye, and cut off your right hand sooner than that these should cause you to fall into sin. Do not go where you are likely to be tempted. "Well," says one, "but my business calls me into the midst of temptation." I grant you that your business may compel you to go where there are ungodly men, for how could some live at all if they had not to come into contact with the ungodly? They would have to go out of the world. Well, then, if that is your case, put on the whole armor of God and do not go without being prepared to fight the good fight of faith. Set a watch, set a watch, set a watch.

Watch against the beginnings of sin. Remember, Satan never begins where he leaves off; he begins with a little sin, and he goes on to a greater one. When he first tempts men, he does not aim at all he hopes to accomplish, but he tries to draw them aside by little and little, and he works up by degrees to the greater sin he wants them to commit. I do not believe that, at the present time, a Christian man can be too precise. We serve a very precise God: "The Lord thy God is a jealous God." Keep out of many things in which professing Christians now indulge themselves. The question is whether they are Christians at all. If we must not judge them, at any rate let us judge for ourselves and settle it once for all, that we dare not go where they go; indeed, we have no wish to do so.

Watch for what God has to say to you. In your reading of the Bible, if the Holy Spirit applies a text of Scripture to you with special force, regard it as a hint from your heavenly Father that there is a lesson in it for you. I am surprised at the way in which the morning text will often instruct me through the whole day. Persons who come to hear the Word of God preached often find that, within two or three days, there is a reason why the preacher delivered that particular sermon and a reason why they were led to hear it.

Whenever you see a professing Christian going astray from the way of holiness, do not talk about it and so increase the mischief. "It is an ill bird that fouls its own nest." Instead of speaking of another's fall, set a watch for yourself, and say, "That is where he slipped, and that is where I may stumble if the grace of God does not keep me." Remember our Savior's words to the three disciples with Him in Gethsemane, "Watch and pray, that ye enter not into temptation."

The Two Guards Together:
Praying and Watching

Dear friends, neither of these two guards is sufficient alone. Prayer alone will not avail. To pray and not to watch is presumption. You pretend to trust in God, and yet you are throwing yourself into danger, as the Devil would have had Christ do when he tempted Him to cast Himself down from a pinnacle of the temple. If you pray to be kept, then be watchful.

Prayer without watchfulness is hypocrisy. A man prays to be kept from sin and then goes into temptation; his prayer is evidently a mere piece of mockery for he does not carry it out in his practice.

Sometimes, however, ignorance may lead to prayer without watching. There are other things that ought not to be omitted. Let me tell you a simple story. There was a little school girl who did not often know her lessons, and there was another girl who sat near her who always said her lessons correctly. Her companion said to her, "Jane, how is it that you always know your lessons?" Jane replied, "I pray to God to help me, and so I know them." The next day the other little girl stood up, but she did not know her lesson; afterward she said to her friend, "I prayed to God about my lesson, but I did not know it any better than I did yesterday." Jane said, "But did you try to learn the lesson?" "No," she said; "I prayed about it, and I thought that was sufficient." Of course she did not know her lesson without learning it. In the same manner, you must watch as well as pray. There must be the daily guard set upon tongue and thought and hand, or else prayer will be in vain.

I have known some people run great risks and yet say that they have prayed to the Lord to preserve them. I have heard, dozens of times, these words, "I made it a matter of prayer," and I have been ready to grow angry with the man who has uttered them. He has done a wrong thing, and he has excused himself because he says that he made it a matter of prayer. A young man married an ungodly young woman, and yet he said that he made it a matter of prayer. A Christian woman married an ungodly man, and when someone blamed her for disobeying the Word of God, she said that she made it a matter of prayer! If you had really sought divine guidance, you would not have dared to do what the

Scriptures expressly forbid to a child of God. Prayer without watching is not sufficient to preserve us from evil.

On the other hand, dear friends, watching without praying is equally futile. To say, "I will keep myself right," and never pray to God to keep you, is self-confidence, which must lead to evil. If you try to watch and do not pray, you will go to sleep, and there will be an end to your watching. It is only by praying and watching that you will be able to keep on your guard. Besides, watching grows wearisome without prayer, and we soon give it up unless we have a sweet interlude of prayer to give us rest and to help us to continue watching.

I will not keep you longer when I have said this: put the two together, watch and pray, or, as my text has it, pray and watch. One will help the other. Prayer will call out the watchman, prayer will incite him to keep his eyes open, prayer will be the food to sustain him during the night, prayer will be the fire to warm him. On the other hand, watching will help prayer, for watching proves prayer to be true. Watching excites prayer, for every enemy we see will move us to pray more earnestly. Moreover, watching is prayer. If there be true watching, the watching itself is prayer. The two blend one into the other. Beloved friends, I send you away with my text ringing in your ears, "We made our prayer unto our God, and set a watch against them day and night."

But I have not been speaking to all who are here. Some of you do not pray, some of you cannot set a watch. The message for you is, "Ye must be born again." You cannot attempt Christian duties until first you have the Christian life, and the only way to get the Christian life is to have faith in the Lord Jesus Christ. Come to the fountain that He has filled with His precious blood; wash there and be clean; then, quickened by His Spirit, set a watch. I am looking to see some souls brought to Christ at this service, for although I have been preaching to God's people, if they will watch for you and pray for you, there will come a blessing to you through their watching and their praying. The Lord grant that it may come to many of you! "Seek ye the Lord while he may be found, call ye upon him while he is near." May many seek and find the Lord tonight, and may many call upon Him in truth! "Whosoever shall call on the name of the Lord shall be saved." God grant that it may be so to everybody here, for Jesus' sake! Amen.

5

The Young Man's Prayer

O satisfy us early with thy mercy; that we may rejoice and be glad all our days (Psalm 90:14).

Israel had suffered a long night of affliction. Dense was the darkness while they abode in Egypt, and cheerless was the glimmering twilight of that wilderness that was covered with their graves. Amid a thousand miracles of mercy, what must have been the sorrows of a camp in which every halt was marked with many burials, until the whole track was a long cemetery? I suppose that the mortality in the camp of Israel was never less than fifty each day—if not three times that number—so that they learned experimentally that verse of the psalm, "For we are consumed by thine anger, and by thy wrath are we troubled." Theirs was the weary march of men who wander about in search of tombs; they traveled toward a land that they could never reach, weary with a work the result of which only their children should receive. You may easily understand how these troubled ones longed for the time when the true day of Israel should dawn, when the black midnight of Egypt and the dark twilight of the wilderness should both give way to the rising sun of the settled rest in Canaan. Most fitly was the prayer offered by Moses—the representative man of all that host—"O satisfy us early with thy mercy"; hasten the time when we shall come to our promised rest; bring on speedily the season when we shall sit under our own vines and our own fig trees, "and shall rejoice and be glad all our days."

This prayer falls from the lips of yonder brother, whose rough pathway for many a mile has descended into the Valley of Deathshade. Loss after loss has he experienced, until as in Job's case, the messengers of evil have trodden upon one another's heels. His griefs are new every morning, and his trials fresh every evening. Friends forsake him and

---

This sermon was taken from *The Metropolitan Tabernacle Pulpit* and was preached on Sunday morning, June 7, 1863.

prove to be deceitful brooks; God breaks him with a tempest; he finds no pause in the ceaseless shower of his troubles. Nevertheless, his hope is not extinguished, and his constant faith lays hold upon the promise that "weeping may endure for a night, but joy cometh in the morning." He understands that God will not always chide, neither does He keep His anger forever; therefore he watches for deliverance even as they that watch for the morning, and his most appropriate cry is, "O satisfy us early with thy mercy"; lift up the light of Your countenance upon us, show Your marvelous lovingkindness in this present hour of need. O my God, make haste to help me, be a very present help in time of trouble; fly to my relief lest I perish from the land; awake for my rescue that I may rejoice and be glad all my days.

See yonder sick bed! Tread lightly, lest perchance you disturb the brief slumbers of that daughter of affliction. She has tossed to and fro days and nights without number, counting her minutes by her pains, and numbering her hours with the paroxysms of her agony. From that couch of suffering where many diseases have conspired to torment the frail body of this child of woe, where the soul itself has grown weary of life and longs for the wings of a dove, I think this prayer may well arise, "O satisfy us early with thy mercy." When will the eternal day break upon my long night? When will the shadows flee away? Sweet Sun of Glory! when will You rise with healing beneath Your wings? I shall be satisfied when I wake up in Your likeness, O Lord; hasten that joyful hour; give me a speedy deliverance from my bed of weakness that I may rejoice and be glad throughout eternal days.

I think the prayer would be equally appropriate from many a distressed conscience where conviction of sin has rolled heavily over the soul until the bones are sore vexed, and the spirit is overwhelmed. That poor heart indulges the hope that Jesus Christ will one day comfort it and become its salvation; it has a humble hope that these woundings will not last forever but shall all be healed by mercy's hand; that He who loosens the bands of Orion will one day deliver the prisoner out of his captivity. Oh! conscience-stricken sinner, you may on your knees now cry out—"O satisfy me early with Your mercy; keep me not always in this house of bondage; let me not plunge forever in this slough of despond; set my feet upon a rock; wash me from my iniquities; clothe me with garments of salvation, and put the new song into my mouth, that I may rejoice and be glad all my days."

Still it appears to me that without straining so much as one word even in the slightest degree, I may take my text this morning as the prayer of a young heart, expressing its desire for present salvation. To you, young men and maidens, shall I address myself, and may the good Spirit cause you in the days of your youth to remember your Creator, while the evil days come not, nor the years draw nigh when you shall say, we have no pleasure in them. I hope the angel of the Lord has said to me, "Run, speak to that young man," and that like the good housewife in the Proverbs, I shall have a portion also for the maidens!

I shall use the text in two ways; first, *as the ground of my address to the young*; and then, secondly, *as a model for your address to God.*

Give Your Hearts to Christ

The voice of wisdom reminds you in this our text that you are not pure in God's sight, but *need His mercy*. Early as it is with you, you must come before God on the same footing as those who seek Him at the eleventh hour. Here is nothing said about merit, nothing concerning the natural innocency of youth and the beauty of the juvenile character. You are not thus flattered and deceived; Holy Scripture guides you aright by dictating to you an evangelical prayer such as God will deign to accept—"O satisfy us early *with thy mercy*." Young man, though as yet no outward crimes have stained your character, yet your salvation must be the work of reigning grace, and that for several reasons. *Your nature is at the present moment full of sin and saturated with iniquity*, and hence you are the object of God's most righteous anger. How can He meet an heir of wrath on terms of justice? His holiness cannot endure you. What if you be made an heir of glory, will not this be grace and grace alone? If ever you are made meet to be a partaker with the saints in light, this must surely be love's own work. Inasmuch as your nature, altogether apart from your actions, deserves God's reprobation, it is mercy that spares you, and if the Lord be pleased to renew your heart, it will be to the praise of the glory of His grace. Be not proud, repel not this certain truth, that you are an alien, a stranger, an enemy, born in sin and shapen in iniquity, by nature an heir of wrath, even as others; yield to its force and seek that mercy that is as really needed by you as by the hoary-headed villain who rots into His grace festering with debauchery and lust.

Besides, your conscience reminds you that your outward life *has not been what it should be*. How soon did we begin to sin! While we were yet little children we went astray, from the womb speaking lies. How rebellious we were! How we chose our own will and way and would by no means submit ourselves to our parents! How in our riper youth we thought it sport to scatter firebrands and carry the hot coals of sin in our bosoms! We played with the serpent, charmed with its azure scales, but forgetful of its poisoned fangs. Far be it from us to boast with the Pharisee—"Lord, I thank thee that I am not as others"; but rather let the youngest pray with the publican—"God be merciful to me a sinner." A little child but seven years of age cried when under conviction of sin—

"Can the Lord have mercy upon such a great sinner as I am, who have lived seven years without fearing and loving Him?" Ah! my friends, if this babe could thus lament, what should be the repentance of those who are fifteen, or sixteen, or seventeen, or eighteen, or twenty, or who have passed the year of manhood. What shall you say, since you have lived so long wasting your precious days—more priceless than pearls—neglecting those golden years, despising divine things, and continuing in rebellion against God? Lord, You know that young though we be, we have multitudes of sins to confess, and therefore it is mercy, mercy, mercy that we crave at Your hands. Remember, beloved young friends, that if you be saved in the morning of life, *you will be wonderful instances of preventing mercy.* It is great mercy that blots out sin, but who shall say that it is not equally great mercy that prevents it? To bring home yonder sheep that has long gone astray, with its wool all torn, its flesh bleeding, and its bones broken, manifests the tender care of the good Shepherd; but, oh! to reclaim the lamb at the commencement of its strayings, to put it into the fold, to keep it there, and to nurture it. What a million mercies are here compressed into one!

To pluck the seared brand from out of the fire when it is black and scorched with the flame—there are depths of mercy here; but are there not heights of love when the young wood is planted in the courts of the Lord and made to flourish as a cedar? However soon we are saved, the glory of perfection has departed from us, but how happy is he who tarries but a few years in a state of nature, as if the fall and the rising again walked hand in hand. No soul is without spot or wrinkle, but some stains are spots the young believer is happily delivered from. Habits of vice and continuance in crime he has not known. He never knew the drunkard's raging thirst; the black oath of the swearer never cancered his mouth. This younger son has not been long in the far country; he comes back before he has long fed the swine. He has been black in the sight of God, but in the eyes of men and in the open vision of onlookers, the young believer seems as if he had never gone astray. Here is great mercy, mercy for which heaven is to be praised forever and ever. This, I think, I may call *distinguishing grace,* with an emphasis. All election distinguishes, and all grace is discriminating, but that grace which adopts the young child so early is distinguishing in the highest degree. As Jenubath, the young son of Hadad, was brought up in the court of Pharaoh and weaned in the king's palace, so are some saints sanctified from the womb. Happy is it for any young man, an elect one out of the elect is he, if he be weaned upon the knees of piety and handled upon the lap of holiness, if he be lighted to his bed with the lamps of the sanctuary and lulled to his sleep with the name of Jesus! If I may breathe a prayer in public for my children, let them be clothed with a little ephod, like young Samuel, and nourished in the chambers of the temple, like the young prince Joash. O my dear young friends, it is mercy, mercy in a distinguishing and peculiar degree, to be saved early, because of your fallen nature, because of sin committed, and yet more because of sin prevented and distinguishing favor bestowed.

But I have another reason for endeavoring to plead with the young this morning, hoping that the Spirit of God will plead with them. I remark that salvation, if it comes to you, must not only be mercy, *but it must be mercy through the Cross*. I infer that from the text, because the text desires it to be a satisfying mercy, and there is no mercy which ever can satisfy a sinner but mercy through the Cross of Christ. Many preach a mercy apart from the Cross. Many say that God is merciful, and therefore surely He will not condemn them, but in the pangs of death and in the terrors of conscience, the uncovenanted mercy of God is no solace to the soul. Some proclaim a mercy that is dependent upon human effort, human goodness, or merit, but no soul ever yet did or could find any lasting satisfaction in this delusion. Mercy by mere ceremonies, mercy by outward ordinances, is but a mockery of human thirst. Like Tantalus, who is mocked by the receding waters, so is the ceremonialist who tries to drink where he finds all comfort flying from him. Young man, the Cross of Christ has that in it which can give you solid, satisfying comfort if you put your trust in it. It can satisfy *your judgment*. What is more logical than the great doctrine of substitution? God so terribly just that He will by no means spare the guilty, and that justice is wholly met by Him who stood in the room, place, and stead of His people! Here is that which will satisfy your *conscience*. Your conscience knows that God must punish you; it is one of those truths that God stamped upon it when He first made you what you are; but when your soul sees Christ punished instead of you, it pillows its head right softly. There is no resting place for conscience but at the Cross. Priests may preach what they will, and philosophers may imagine what they please, but there is in the conscience of man, in its unrestingness, an indication that the Cross of Christ must have come from God, because that conscience never ceases from its disquiet until it hides in the wounds of the Crucified. Never again shall conscience alarm you with dreadful thoughts of the wrath to come, if you lay hold of that mercy which is revealed in Jesus Christ. Here, too, is satisfaction *for all your fears*. Do they pursue you today like a pack of hungry dogs in full pursuit of the stag? Fly to Christ and your fears have vanished! What has that man to fear for whom Jesus died? Need he alarm himself when Christ stands in his stead before the eternal throne and pleads there for him? Here, too, is satisfaction *for your hopes*. He that gets Christ gets all the future wrapped up in Him. There are also peace and joy and safety for all the years and for all the eternity to come in the same Christ Jesus who has put away your sin. Oh! I would young man, I would young woman, that you would put your trust in Jesus now, for in Him there is an answer to this prayer—"O satisfy us early with thy mercy."

Furthermore, anxiously would I press this matter of a youthful faith upon you, *because you have a dissatisfaction even now.* Do I not speak the truth when, looking into the bright eyes of the happiest among you, I venture to say that you are not perfectly satisfied. You feel that something is lacking. My lad, your boyish games cannot quite satisfy you; there is a something in you more noble than toys and games can gratify. Young man, your pursuits of business furnish you with some considerable interest and amusement, but still there is an aching void—you know there is—and although pleasure promises to fill it, you have begun already to discover that you have a thirst that is not to be quenched with water, and a hunger that is not to be satisfied with bread. You know it is so. The other evening when you were quite alone, when you were quietly thinking matters over, you felt that this present world was not enough for you. The majesty of a mysterious longing that God had put in you lifted up itself and claimed to be heard! Did it not? The other day, after the party was over at which you had so enjoyed yourself, when it was all done and everybody was gone and you were quite quiet, did you not feel that even if you had these things every day of your life, yet you could not be content? You want you know not what, but something you do want to fill your heart. We look back upon our younger days and think that they were far happier than our present state, and we sometimes fancy that we used to be satisfied then, but I believe that our thoughts imagine a great falsehood. I do from my soul confess that I never was satisfied until I came to Christ; when I was yet a child I had far more wretchedness than ever I have now; I will even add, more weariness, more care, more heartache, than I know at this day. I may be singular in this confession, but I make it and know it to be the truth. Since that dear hour when my soul cast itself on Jesus, I have found solid joy and peace, but before that all those supposed thrills of early youth, all the imagined ease and joy of boyhood, were but vanity and vexation of spirit to me. You do feel, if I know anything about you, that you are not quite satisfied now. Well, then, let me say to you again, that I would have you come to Jesus, for depend upon it there is that in Him which can thoroughly satisfy you.

What can you want more to satisfy *your heart* than love to Him? Our hearts all crave for an object upon which they may be set. We often surrender ourselves to an unworthy object that betrays us or proves too narrow to accommodate our hearts' desire. But if you love Jesus, you will love one who deserves your warmest affection, who will amply repay your fullest confidence, and who will never betray it. You say that not only does your heart want something, but your *head*. My witness is that there is in the Gospel of Christ the richest food for the brain. Before you know Christ you read, you search, you study, and you put what you learn into a wild chaos of useless confusion; after you have found Christ, everything else that you learn is put in its proper place. You get Christ as the central sun, and then every science and fact begins to revolve round about Him just as the planets travel in their perpetual circle around the central orb. Without Christ we are ignorant, but with Him we understand the most excellent of sciences, and all others shall fall into their proper place.

This is an age when, without a true faith in Christ, the young mind has a dreary pilgrimage before it. False guides are standing arrayed in all sorts of garb, ready to lead you first to doubt this book of Scripture, then to distrust the whole, then to mistrust God and Christ, and then to doubt your own existence and to come into the dreary dreamland where nothing is certain, but where everything is myth and fiction. Give your heart to Christ, young man, and He will furnish you with anchors and good anchor-hold to your mind, so that when stormy winds of skepticism sweep across the sea and other barks are wrecked, you shall outride the storm and shall evermore be safe. It is a strange thing that people should be so long before they are satisfied. Look at some of my hearers today. They meant to be satisfied with money, and when they earned journeymen's wages, they came to be journeymen, and then they were not satisfied until they were foremen; then they felt they never should be satisfied until they had a concern of their own. They got a concern of their own and took a house in the city, but then they felt they could not be content until they had taken the adjoining premises; they had more advertising and more work to do, and then they began to feel that they never would be quite easy until they have purchased a snug little villa in the country. Yes, there are some here who had the villa, handsome grounds, and so on, but they will not be satisfied until they see all their children married; when they have seen all their children married, they will not be at rest then; they think they will, but they will not. There is always a something yet beyond. "Man never is, but always to be blessed," as Young puts it.

There are Fortunate Isles for the mariner to reach, and failing these there is no haven for him even in the safest port. We know some, too, who instead of pursuing wealth, are looking after fame. They have been honored for that clever piece of writing, but they are emulous of more honor; they must write better still; and when they have achieved some degree of notoriety through a second attempt, they will feel that now they have a name to keep up, and they must have that name widened, and the circle of their influence must extend. The fact is, that neither wealth, nor honor, nor anything that is of mortal birth can ever fill the insatiable, immortal soul of man. The heart of man has an everlasting hunger given to it, and if you could put worlds into its mouth, it would still crave for more; it is so thirsty that if all the rivers drained themselves into it, still, like the deep sea which is never full, the heart would yet cry out for more. Man is truly like the horseleech; ever he says, "Give! give! give!" and until the Cross be given to the insatiable heart, until Jesus Christ, who is the fullness of Him that fills all in all, be bestowed, the heart of man never can be full.

Where shall we find a satisfied man but in the church of Christ? And in the church of Christ I find him, not in the pulpit merely, where success and position might satisfy, but I find him in the pew humbly receiving the truth. I find him in the pew, not among the rich where earthly comforts might tend to make him satisfied, but among the poor where cold and nakedness might cause him to complain. I could point you today to the workman who earns every bit of bread he eats with more sweat of his brow than you would dream of, but he is content. I could point you to the poor work girl who scarce earns enough to hold body and soul together, and yet in this house of God her heart often leaps for joy, for she is wholly resigned. I could show you the bedridden woman whose bones come through the skin through long lying upon a bed that friendship would fain make soft, but that is all too hard for her weakness, and yet she is content, though a parish pittance be all that is given her to feed upon. I say we have no need to exaggerate or strain or use hyperboles; we do find in the church of Christ those who have been and still are satisfied with the mercy of God. Now, would it not be a fine thing to begin life with being satisfied? There are some who do not end it with this attainment; they hunt after satisfaction until they come to their dying beds, and then do not find it at last. But it would be a fine thing to begin life with being satisfied, not to say, at some future date I will be satisfied, but to be content now; not when I have climbed to such-and-such a pinnacle I shall have enough, but to have enough now, to begin with satisfaction before you launch upon a world of troubles! You may do so, my brother; you may do so, my young sister, if now with a true heart you look to Him who hangs upon yonder cross, and commit your soul into His keeping, praying this prayer—"O satisfy us *early* with thy mercy."

The reason that our text gives I must comment upon for a moment. Our text says—"O satisfy us early with thy mercy; *that we may rejoice and be glad all our days.*" We never *rejoice* in the true sense of the term; we never possess solid gladness until we are satisfied with God's mercy. It is all a mockery and a pretense; the reality never comes to us until

God's mercy visits our hearts; after that what joy we know! Tell me that the Christian is miserable! O sir, you do not know what the Christian is. We need not appear before you with laughing faces, for our joy is deeper than yours and needs not to tell itself out in immodest signs. The poor trader puts all his goods in the window, but the rich man has rich stores even in the dark cellar; his warehouses are full, and he makes no show. Still waters run deep, and we are sometimes still in our joy because of the depth of our delight. Say we are not happy! Sirs, we would not change one moment of our joy for a hundred years of yours! We hear your joy, and we understand that it is like the crackling of thorns under a pot that crackle all the louder because they burn so furiously and will so soon be gone. But ours is a steady fire. We do mourn sometimes; we mourn more often than we ought to do. We are free to confess this. But it is not our religion that makes us mourn; it is because we do not live up to it, for when we live up to it and have the company of Jesus.

Our sickbeds are often as the doorstep of heaven even when we are cast down; there is a sweet solace in our sorrow and a profound joy about our apparent grief that we would not give away; God gave it to us and the world cannot destroy it. They who love Jesus Christ early have the best hope of enjoying the happiest days as Christians. *They will have the most service*, and the service of God is perfect delight. Their youthful vigor will enable them to do more than those who enlist when they are old and decrepit. The joy of the Lord is our strength; on the other hand, to use our strength for God is a fountain of joy. Young man, if you give fifty years of service to God, surely you shall rejoice all your days. The earlier we are converted, having the longer time to study in Christ's college, *the more profound shall be our knowledge of Him*. We shall have more time for communion, more years for fellowship. We shall have more seasons to prove the power of prayer, and more opportunities to test the fidelity of God than we should if we came late. Those who come late are blessed by being helped to learn so much, but those that come in early shall surely outstrip them. Let me be young, like John, that I may have years of loving service, and like him may have much of intimate acquaintance with my Lord. Surely those who are converted early may reckon upon more joy because *they never will have to contend with and to mourn over what later converts must know*. Your bones are not broken, you can run without weariness, you have not fallen as some have done, you can walk without fainting. Often the gray-headed man who is converted at sixty or seventy finds the remembrance of his youthful sins clinging to him. When he would praise, an old lascivious song revives upon his memory; when he would mount up to heaven, he suddenly remembers some scene in a haunt of vice which he would be glad to forget. But you, saved by divine grace before you thus fall into the jaw of the lion or under the paw of the bear, will certainly have cause for rejoicing all your life. If I may have heavenly music upon earth, let me begin it now, Lord. Put not away the viol and the harp for my fingers when they tremble with age; let me use them while yet I am young. Now, Lord, if there be a banquet, do not bring me in at the end of the feast, but let me begin to feast today. If I am to be married to Jesus, let it not be when my hair is gray, but marry me to Jesus now. What better time for joy than today? Now shall my joys swell and grow like a river that rolls on to a mightier breadth and depth as its course is prolonged! I shall rejoice and be glad in You all my days, good Lord, if You will now begin with me in this the morning of my days.

I cannot put my thoughts together this morning as I could desire, but I still feel an earnest longing to shoot the arrow to its mark, and therefore, one or two stray thoughts before I turn to the prayer itself and these shall be very brief. My dear young friends, you who are of my own age, or younger still, I beseech you ask to be satisfied with God's mercy early *for you may die early.* It has been our grief this week to stand by the open grave of one who was, alas! too soon, as we thought, snatched away to heaven. You may never number the full ripe years of manhood. We say that our years are threescore and ten, but to you they may not even be a score; your sun may go down while it is yet noon. God often reaps His corn green; long before the autumn comes He cuts down His sheaves. "Because I will do this . . . , prepare to meet thy God." Then, on the other hand, if you should live, *in whose service could you spend your days better than in the service of God?* What more happy employment, what more blessed position than to be found, like Samuel, a servant waiting upon God while yet you need a mother's care. *Remember how early temptations beset you.* Would you not wish to secure your early days? And how can you cleanse your ways except by taking heed to them according to God's Word? Do you not know, too, *that the church wants you?* Your young blood shall keep her veins full of vigor and make her sinews strong. *Should not the love of Jesus Christ win you?* If He died and shed His blood for men, does He not deserve their best service? Would you desire to give to God an offering of only the end of your days? What would you have thought of the Jew who brought an old bullock—who after having used an ox in his own fields until it was worn out should then consecrate it to God? Let the lambs be offered; let the firstlings of the herd be brought; let God have the first sheaves of the harvest. Surely He deserves something better than to have the Devil's leavings put upon His holy altar! "Oh! but," you say, "would He accept me if I came to Him early?" Why, you have more promises than the old man has. It is written that God will be found of them that seek Him, but it is specially written, "They that seek me early shall find me." You have a peculiar promise given to you. If there were any who could be rejected, it could not by any possibility be the young. If there were one whom Jesus Christ could leave, it would not be you, for He gathers the lambs in His bosom. "Suffer the little children to come unto me, and forbid them not, for of such is the kingdom of heaven." May not that cheer you, however young you be? Jesus Christ loves to see young men and maidens join in His praise. We find that the best of saints in the Old and New Testament were those who came to Jesus young. Certain it is that the pick and cream of the church in modern times will be found among those who are early converts. Look at those who are church officers and ministers, and in most cases the leaders in our Israel are those who, as young Hannibal was devoted by his parents to the great cause of his country, were devoted by their parents to the great cause of Zion and to the interests of Jerusalem. If you would be strong for God, eminent in His service, and joyful in His ways, if you would understand the heights and depths of the love of Christ which passes knowledge, if you would give yourself before your bones are broken and before your spirit has become tinctured through and through with habits of iniquity, then offer this prayer—"O satisfy us early with thy mercy; that we may rejoice and be glad all our days."

Make Your Address to God

Every word here is significant. "*O.*" This teaches us *that the prayer is to be earnest.* I will suppose that I have led some of you young people here now to breathe this prayer to God. Am I so unhappy as to suppose that none of you will do it? Are there not some who now say, "I will with my whole heart, God the Holy Spirit helping me, now in my pew offer this supplication to heaven"? It begins with an "O." Dull prayers will never reach God's throne. What comes from your heart coldly can never get to God's heart. Dull, dead prayers—ask God to deny them. We must pray out of our very souls. The soul of our prayer must be the prayer of our soul. "*O* satisfy us." Young man, the Lord is willing to open the door to those who knock, but you must knock hard. He is fully prepared to give to those who ask, but you must ask earnestly. The kingdom of heaven suffers violence. It is not a gentle grasp that will avail; you must *wrestle* with the angel. Give no sleep to your eyes nor slumber to your eyelids until you have found the Savior. Remember, if you do but find Him, it will well repay you though you shed drops of blood in the pursuit. If instead of tears you had given your heart's gore, and if instead of sighs you were to give the shrieks of a martyr, it would well recompense you if you did but find Jesus; therefore be earnest. If you find Him not, remember, you perish, and perish with a great destruction; the wrath of God abides on you, and hell must be your portion; therefore as one that pleads for his life, so plead for mercy. Throw your whole spirit into it, and let that spirit be heated to a glowing heat. Be not satisfied to stand at the foot of the throne and say, "Let God save me if He will." No, but put it thus, "Lord, I cannot take a denial; O satisfy me; O save me." Such a prayer is sure to be accepted.

Again, *make it a generous prayer* when you are at it. "O satisfy *us* early!" I am glad to see among our young sisters in the catechumen class such a spirit of love for one another, so that when one is converted she is sure to look around for another; the scores in that class who have found the Lord are always searching out some stray young woman in the street or some hopeful ones attending the congregation whom they try to bring in that Jesus may be glorified. The very first duty of a convert is to labor for the conversion of others, and surely it will not spoil your prayer, young man, if when you are praying for yourself you will put it in the plural—"O satisfy *us*." Pray for your brothers and sisters. I am sure we are verily guilty in this thing. Those that sprang from the same loins as ourselves—would to God that they were all saved with the same salvation. You may, some of you, be happy enough to be members of a family in which all are converted. Oh, that we could all say the same! May the remembrance of this text provoke you and me to pray for unconverted brothers and sisters more than we have ever done. "O satisfy *us;*" if You have brought in the eldest, Lord, stay not until the youngest be converted; if my brother preaches the Word, if my sister rejoices in Your fear, then let other sisters know and taste of Your love. You young people in shops, in warehouses, in factories, pray this prayer, and do not exclude even those who have begun to blaspheme, but even in their early youth pray for them—"O satisfy *us* with thy mercy."

See to it, dear friends, in the next place *that your prayer be thoroughly evangelical.* "O satisfy us early with thy mercy." The prayer of the publican is the model for us all. No matter how amiable or how excellent we may be, we must each come and say, "God, be merciful to me a sinner." Do not come with any hereditary godliness; do not approach the Lord with the fact of your infant sprinkling; do not come before Him to plead your mother's covenant. Come as a sinner, as a foul, filthy sinner having nothing to rely on or to trust to but the merit of God in Christ Jesus; let the prayer be just such as a thief might offer or a prostitute might present—"O satisfy us early with thy mercy."

Let the prayer be put up now *at once.* The text says, "O satisfy us early." Why not today? Oh, that it had been done years ago! But there was time enough, you thought. There is time enough, but there is none to spare. Acquaint yourself *now* with God, and be at peace. "Today is the accepted time; today is the day of salvation." I would to God we would not pray our prayers meaning to have them heard so late. Let it be—"O satisfy us early." The man who truly repents always wants to have pardon on the spot; he feels as if he could not rise from his knees until God has been favorable to him. Mark you, when a man has really come to that point that he must be saved now, or else he feels that it will be too late, then has come the solemn juncture when God will say—"Be it unto thee even as thou wilt."

I must leave this poor sermon of mine with the people of God, to pray over it. Sometimes when most I long to plead with men's sons, I find the brain distracted although the heart is warm. God knows could I plead with the young, I would do it even to tears. I do feel it such a solemn thing for our country. Happy shall she be if her sons and daughters give their young days to God! It will be such a blessed thing for London if our young men in business and our young women in families become missionaries for Christ. But what a happy thing it will be for them! What joy shall they know! What transports shall they feel! What a blessing will they be to their households! What happy families they will be! Unconverted fathers shall be made to feel the power of godliness through their daughters, and mothers who despise religion shall not dare to negelct it any longer because they see it exemplified and illustrated in their sons. We want missionaries everywhere. This great city never can by any possibility become the Lord's except by individual action. We must have all Christians at work, and since we cannot get the old ones to work as we would, since preach as we may, they will settle on their lees, we long for new recruits whose ardor shall rekindle the dying enthusiasm of the seniors. We want to see fresh minds come in all aglow with holy fervor to keep the fire still blazing on the altar. For Jesus Christ's sake I do implore you, you who number but few years, offer this supplication in your pew. Do it now. It is a brother's heart that begs the favor. It is for your own soul's sake, that you may be blessed on earth, and that you may have the joys of heaven. There is a prayer-hearing God. The mercy seat is still open. Christ still waits. May the Spirit of God compel you now to come before Him in supplication. Now may He compel you to come in with this as your cry—"O satisfy us early with thy mercy; that we may rejoice and be glad all our days."

6

The Student's Prayer

Make me to understand the way of thy precepts: so shall I talk of thy wondrous works (Psalm 119:27).

When we seek any good thing from God, we ought also to consider how we may use it for His glory. It is meet that desires for good things should flow from good motives. When the heart is not only gracious but grateful, it will turn to God with double purpose, desiring the mercy and desiring to use it to His praise. The grace of God, which brings salvation, does marvelously whet the appetite for good things; it does more, it provokes an intense anxiety to glorify God's name in the world even before it has imparted the ability to do any good thing. Vehement passion and abject helplessness meeting together and struggling in the breast often lead to despondency, but they ought far rather to stimulate prayer.

Directly after we are saved by grace, we are eager after supplies for our soul's wants. "As newborn babes, desire the sincere milk of the word, that ye may grow thereby." This is the first stage of spiritual childhood; like the infant who cries for the bottle and takes its little fill and feasts, all to itself, and all for itself. There follows on this another yearning, a desire for fellowship with the saints, although we feel too weak and too foolish to enter into such good company, as we take the older disciples to be, or even to talk to them. But I will tell you what we can do. We may all venture to ask the Lord to instruct us and make us understand His ways so that our conversation may be welcome to His people, and so He will. "Wherefore comfort yourselves together, and edify one another, even as also ye do." This is the second stage of development. Then comes a third grade, and come it surely will if you follow on to know the Lord. "Then will I teach transgressors thy ways; and sinners

---

This sermon was taken from *The Metropolitan Tabernacle Pulpit* and was preached at the Metropolitan Tabernacle, Newington, in 1877.

shall be converted unto thee." Speak not, my brother, on this wise—
"You have told me, O my God, to covet earnestly the best gifts. I do
covet them, Lord, you know, not to consume them upon my lusts, but to
use them for Your service. I gladly will accept Your talents as a trust, not
to trifle with them, not to vaunt them as the toys of my vanity, but by
your grace as a wise and faithful steward to bring you all the profit and
all the interest, for I am greedy to get gain out of all those endowments
You do entrust to my care." "Make me to understand the way of thy precepts: so shall I talk of thy wondrous works."

I would have you further observe, on the threshold of our meditation,
that there is not really any grave duty a man can be called on to discharge, no responsible office he may be elected to fill, nor even any plan
or purpose he lays it on his heart to accomplish that does not require
diligent preparation on his own part to fit himself, to train his faculties,
and to discipline his mind. What you call unskilled labor may possibly
be utilized by efficient officers, but unskillful labor is a sheer waste of
power. Now much more imperative the demand that we should be endowed with the requisite faculties and qualified by suitable instruction if
we have any work to do for God, or any office, however humble, in the
service of the great King! Zeal without knowledge would only betray us
into reckless presumption. When called to talk of God's wondrous
works, we ought not to rush upon that exercise at once unfitted and unprepared, but we should wait upon the Lord, that the eyes of our understanding may be enlightened, that our stammering tongues may be
unloosed, and that our lips may be attuned to tell the noble tale in grateful strains. We must first obtain for ourselves an understanding of the
way of the Lord's precepts before we can make it plain to others. He
who tries to teach, but has never been taught himself, will make a sorry
mess of it. He who has no understanding, and yet wants to make others
understand, must assuredly fail. Some there are who cannot teach and
will not learn, and it is because they will not learn that they cannot
teach. I believe aptness for being taught is at the bottom of aptness to
teach. The psalmist had both. He says, "Make me to understand the way
of thy statutes." There he would be taught. "Then," says he, "I shall talk
of thy wondrous works." There he would be teaching

In pondering the text, it has appeared to me to set forth three things,
first, *the prayer of the student;* secondly, *the occupation of the scholar;*
and thirdly, *the intimate relation there is between them.*

The Prayer of the Student

I hope, my beloved brethren and sisters in Christ, that we are all stu-
dents in the school of Christ—all disciples, or scholars—and I trust we
shall adopt the student's prayer as our own: "Make me to understand the

way of thy precepts." You know that prayer is to study what fire is to the sacrifice; I beseech you, therefore, join heartily in the petition of the text.

The student's prayer deals with the main subject of the conversation that is to be that student's occupation, namely, *the way of God's precepts*. You and I, brethren, have to teach those things that relate to the counsels and commandments of the Lord. It is not our province to guide men in politics or to tutor them in science. Those things are better taught by men of mark, whose time and attention are absorbed in those profound and laborious researches. As for us who are Christians and servants of Christ, our business is to teach men the things of God. To that one topic we do well to keep, both for our own good and for the good of others. If we have many studies to engage us, our thoughts will soon be scattered; if we multiply our pursuits, we shall be incapable of concentrating all our energies upon the grand topic that divine wisdom has selected for us—"the way of thy precepts."

In the way of God's legal precepts we have great need of sound understanding that we may be competent to instruct others. It is well to be initiated in the law, to discern its wonderful comprehensiveness, spirituality, and severity; to know the way of the law—a way too hard to be trodden by any mortal man so as to win salvation thereby. It is well to survey the way of the Lord's precepts, to see how exceedingly broad and yet at the same time how remarkably narrow it is, for "thy commandment is exceeding broad," and yet "strait is the gate, and narrow is the way, which leadeth unto life, and few there be that find it." It is well for us to know exactly what the law teaches and what the law designs, why we were made subject to its prescript, and how we may be delivered from its penalties.

Great need too have we to understand the way of God's gospel precepts—what these precepts are: "repent," "believe," "be converted," and the like; to be able to see their relation, where they stand, not as means to an end, but as results of divine grace—commands but yet promises, the duty of man but yet the gift of God. Happy is that preacher and teacher who understands the way of the gospel precepts and never lets them clash with the precepts of the law so as to teach a mingle-mangle, half law and half Gospel; who knows the way of God's legal precepts and sees them all ablaze with divine wrath on account of sin and discerns the way of the gospel precepts and sees them all bright and yet all crimson with the precious blood of Him that opened up for us the way of acceptance.

The way of God's precepts! Does not that mean that we ought to be acquainted with the relative position that the precepts occupy? For it is very easy, brethren, unless God gives us understanding, to preach up one precept to the neglect of another. It is possible for a ministry and a teaching to be lopsided, and those who follow it may become rather the caricatures of Christianity than Christians harmoniously proportioned. O Lord, what foolish creatures we are! When You do exhort us one way, we run to such an extreme therein that we forget that You have given us any other counsel than that which is just now ringing in our ears. We have known some commanded to be humble who have bowed down until they have become timorous and desponding. We have known others exhorted to be confident who have gone far beyond a modest courage and have grown so presumptuous that they have presently fallen into gross transgressions. Is fidelity to the truth your cardinal virtue? Take heed of being uncharitable. Is love to God and man your highest aspiration? Beware lest you become the dupe of false apostles and foul hypocrites. Have you clad yourself with zeal as with a garment? Have a care now, lest by one act of indiscretion your garment should be rolled in blood. Oh, how easy it is to exaggerate a virtue until it becomes a vice. A man may look to himself, examine himself, and scrutinize all his actions and motives until he becomes deplorably selfish; or on the other hand a man may look to others, counseling them and cautioning them, preaching to them and praying for them until he grows oblivious of his own estate, degenerates into hypocrisy, and discovers to his surprise that his own heart is not right with God. There is a "way" about the precepts, there is a chime about them in which every bell gives out its note and makes up a tune. There is a mixture, as of old, of the anointing oil—so much of this and that and the other; if any ingredient were left out, the oil would have lost its perfect aroma. So is there an anointing of the holy life in which there is precept upon precept skillfully mingled, delicately infused, gratefully blended, and grace given to keep each of these precepts, and so the life becomes sweet like an ointment most precious to the Lord. God grant us each, if we are to teach others—and I hope we shall all try to do that—to understand the way of His precepts.

As a prayer, too, this must certainly mean, "Make me understand the way to keep thy precepts." It is not in human strength, for he that keeps the precepts of God must be kept by the God of the precepts. To keep the precepts we must keep Him in the heart who gave the precepts and whose life is the best exemplification of them. O Lord, teach us the way to observe and to do Your commands. Give us such humble, dependent hearts, so receptive of the sweet influences of Your Spirit, that we may understand the way in which those precepts are to be kept. Does it not signify—"Lord, make me to understand the Christian life, for that is the way of thy precepts"? Dear friends, if you are teachers of others you must be experimentally acquainted with the Christian life; you must know the great doctrines that support it and furnish motives for it—the great doctrines that are the pavement of the road along which the Christian travels. You must know the practical precepts themselves—what they are and how the Lord has worded them for each circumstance and each age of the Christian life. You must know the doctrinal and the practical, but you must know the experimental. He is no preacher of any value who cannot tell the way of God's precepts by having experienced that way—having felt the joy of running in it—having taken the precepts and been guided by them so as to have proved that "in keeping of them there is great reward." Aye, and he will be none the worse teacher if he has a lively memory of the bitterness that comes of having wandered from those commandments, for he can tell the sinner, with the tear starting to his own eyes, that he who wanders from the way of obedience will miss the paths of peace, for the way of God's commandments is exceedingly pleasant, but they that break the hedge and follow their own will shall find that their willfulness entails upon them grievous sorrow and sore pain. This is what we want—to understand the way of God's precepts. Let the prayer go up to heaven, especially from every young brother who is hoping to preach the Word before long, "Make me to understand the way of thy precepts."

Very obviously here a confession is implied. "Make me to understand the way of thy precepts." It means just this. "Lord, I do not understand it of myself. I am ignorant and foolish, and if I follow my own judgment—if I take to my own thinkings—I shall be sure to go wrong. Lord, make me to understand." It is a confession of a good man who did understand a great deal but felt that he did not understand all. In this learning, he who understands most is the man who thinks he understands least. He who has the clearest knowledge of divine things is the very one to feel that there is a boundless ocean far beyond his observation, and he cries, "Make me to understand the way of thy precepts." It is a confession that should be made because it is intensely felt—the consciousness of folly and ignorance forcing the confession to the lip.

Our student's prayer asks a great boon when he says, "Make me to *understand.*" This is something more than "Make me to *know.*" He had said just before—"Teach me thy statutes." Every Christian needs this teaching for his own sake, but he that is to be an instructor of others must especially inquire for a thorough understanding. You Sunday school teachers who take the oversight of the children and you elders of the church who look after inquirers and help them to the Savior, you must not be satisfied with knowing, you must *understand.* A superficial acquaintance with the Scriptures will not suffice for your important office. Your mind must penetrate into the deeper meaning, the hidden treasures of wisdom. "Make me to *understand.*" A catechism may supply right answers, but we want the living teacher to give us true perceptions.

Intelligence is not a faculty of babes; in understanding be men. Young pupils soon lose confidence in their preceptor if he does not seem up to the mark. I heard two schoolboys talking of their usher the other day. Says one, "I don't think he knows much more than we do." "Well, he always has to look at the book before he can tell us anything, has not he?" said the other little chap. Just now as I came along I watched two babies trying to carry another baby a little smaller than themselves, and they all three rolled down together. It is pretty to see little children anxious to help their little brother, but when the father comes up he lifts all three and carries them with ease. We have not many fathers, but every Christian man should spire to that honorable and valuable estate in the church. The wisdom that comes of experience leads up to it. "Make me to understand." Oh Lord, the children are pleased with the flowers, help me to spy out the roots; take me into the secrets, let me know the deep things of God. Help me to discriminate; enable me to judge and weigh and ponder and so to understand. Such reasons as You give, enable me to comprehend. Where You give no reason teach my reason to feel that there must be the best of reasons for no reasons having been given. So make me to understand what can be understood and to understand that what I cannot understand is just as reliable as what I do understand. In understanding I can never find You out, O God, to perfection. In Your sight I must still be a babe, though toward my fellow Christians I may be a man. "Make me to understand."

I love to meet with those of the Lord's people who have had their senses exercised in divine things and their intelligence matured. For the most part we find disciples like babes, unskillful in the word of righteousness, using milk because unable to digest strong meat. Thank God for the babes, pray God they may soon grow and develop into men. He who knows that he is a sinner and that Christ Jesus is his Savior knows enough to save him. But we have no wish to perpetuate childishness. The spelling book is essential as a primer, but not the spelling book forever! "*A B C*" must not be sung forever in wearisome monotone; nor must "Only Believe" become the everlasting song! Are there not other truths deeper and higher? There is the grand analogy of the faith, there is the doctrine of the covenant, there is the doctrine of election, there is the doctrine of the union of the saints with Jesus Christ. These are the deep things of God, and I think we should pray, "Make me, Lord, to understand them." Yet the best understanding is that which aims at personal holiness. "Make me to understand the *way of thy precepts.*" Lord, if I cannot grapple with doctrine, do let me know which is the right way for me to take in my daily life. If sometimes your truth staggers me, and I cannot see where this truth squares with that, yet Lord, grant that integrity and uprightness may preserve me. So make me to know and understand the way of Your statutes that if I be tempted, and the Tempter come as an angel of light, I may so understand the difference between a true angel of light and the mock angel of light that I may not be taken in the snare. "Make me to understand the way of thy statutes." May my eye be keen to know the right in all its tangles. May I follow the silken clue of uprightness where it seems to wind and twist. Give Your servant such a clear understanding of what Israel ought to do and of what he himself ought to do as a part of Israel that he may never miss his way. This is the best kind of understanding in all the world.

The psalmist appeals to the fountain of all wisdom, the source from whence all knowledge springs. Who can put wisdom in the inward parts but the Lord? Or who can give understanding to the heart but God Most High? Our parents and our Sunday school teachers taught us the rudiments while we were supple and pliant with tender age. We thank them much, and we esteem them highly. Yet they could only teach the law and imprint, if possible, the letter of it on our memories, although even that we often repeated and as often forgot. It is the Lord that teaches us to profit by the divine Spirit. How very wonderfully the Lord does teach us. Some lessons have to be whipped into us. Well, He does not spare the rod for our crying. Other lessons can only be burnt into us as with a hot iron. Some of us can bless the Lord that we bear in our bodies the prints of the Lord Jesus, that He branded His truth into our very flesh and bones, so that we cannot now miss it but must understand it. Into what strange places God will put His children! You have heard of colleges called by odd names—Brasennose, and the like; but the most singular college I ever heard of was the whale's belly. Jonah would never have bowed his self-will to sovereign grace had he not been cast into the deep, compassed about with floods, and overwhelmed with billows and waves. But the soundness of his doctrine was very palpable in the voice of his thanksgiving, for as soon as ever he came out of the whale's belly, he said, "Salvation is of the Lord." A singular college for a prophet, but we may be content to leave the college to God, and if we be like Joseph sold into Egypt or like the Hebrew children carried captive into Babylon or wherever it may be—so long as He makes us to understand the way of His precepts we may be well content. Christ taught only three of His twelve apostles upon Tabor, but eleven of them in Gethsemane. Some, though favored much with high joys, learn more by deep sorrows. He takes but three of them into the chamber where He raises the dead girl, for all His wonders are not to be seen by all His followers; but they may all behold Him on the cross and learn the sweet wonders of His dying love. I would not be satisfied, dear brethren and sisters, without trying to understand all that can be understood of the love of Jesus Christ and of all those precious truths that make up the way of God's precepts. He is a poor scholar who does not wish to learn more than lies within the bare compass of his task; a good pupil will try to get as much as ever he can out of his teacher. Be it your resolve and mine always to be learning! Let us never be content lightly to skim the wave or gently sip the river's brim. Rather let us delight ourselves with diving into the clear stream of knowledge. Revelation invites research, and it unfolds its choice stores only to those who search for them as for hidden treasures. Oh, my God! I long to glean, to gather, to gain knowledge. I would fain yield up every hour I have to sit at Your feet. To You I would surrender every faculty I have that I may be learning. By the ear, by the eye, by the taste would I imbibe instruction; yes, and in every season of recreation I would inhale the fragrance of Your wondrous works; and when I seek repose I would lean my head upon Your bosom that I may learn Your love by the touch as well as by every other sense. May each gate of Mansoul be filled with the traffic of the precious merchandise of heavenly knowledge. And, Lord, I would open the inmost depth of my soul that Your light may shine into the most secret parts of my nature. Oh, hear my cry! Make me to understand the way of Your precepts!

The Occupation of the Scholar

When the Lord has taught a man the way of His precepts, it behooves him rightly to use his sacred privileges: "So shall I talk of thy wondrous works." As a faithful teacher let him testify of *God's works*—His wondrous works. It is a sorry sermon that is all about man's works, especially if the preacher makes out our good works to be something very remarkable. We are to preach not man's works but God's works—not our own works but the works of our great Substitute. There are two works, especially, that you Christian people must talk about to others—the work of Christ *for* us and the work of the Holy Spirit *in* us. These are themes that will never be exhausted. The work of God the Son for us in His life and death, resurrection and ascension, His intercession at the right hand of God and His second advent—what a theme is before you here! How great are the works of Christ on our behalf! Preach His substitution emphatically. Let there be no mistake about that. Let it be told that Christ stood in the place and stead of His people and lived and died for them. Moreover, there is the work of the Holy Spirit *in* us—the vital interest and importance of which it would not be possible to exaggerate. I should not like any man to try and talk about this divine ministry unless he has been brought under its power and been led by experience to understand it—the work of conviction, the work of regeneration, the work of emptying, humbling, and bringing down, the work of leading to repentance and to faith, the work of sanctification, the work of daily sustenance of the divine life, the work of perfecting the soul for heaven.

There is plenty of room for blundering here if God does not make you to understand the way of His precepts! But if you have a good clear knowledge of what Christian life is, then, my dear brothers and sisters, always be dwelling on these two things—what the Lord has done *for* us and what the Lord is doing in us when He brings us out of darkness to His marvelous light.

The wonderful character of these works of God opens up a study on which the devout mind can descant with ever awakening emotions of awe and delight. There are a few things in the world that men may wonder at. They used to speak of the seven wonders of the world. I believe that there is not one of those seven wonders that some have not ceased to wonder at. If you see them a sufficient number of times you get accustomed to them, and the wonder evaporates. But the works of the Lord, and these two works especially, you may think on them, meditate upon them, inspect them, enjoy them every day of a long life, and the result will be not a diminution but an increase of your wonder. "Thy wondrous works!" God incarnate in the Son of Mary! Wondrous work, this! God in the carpenter's shop! The Son of God driving nails and handling a hammer! Wondrous work, this! Jesus at the loom, weaving a righteousness for His people, casting His soul into every throw of the shuttle and producing such a matchless fabric for the wedding dress of His own chosen bride that all the angels in heaven stand still and gaze at it and marvel how such a fabric was wrought! Behold Him—God Himself in human flesh—dying, bearing human sin with a condescension that is wonderful beyond all wonder! Behold Him casting all that sin into the depth of the sea with wondrous might of merit that drowned it in the bottomless abyss for aye! Wondrous work, that! Then see Him going forth again, discharged from all His suretyship engagements, having paid the debt; behold Him nailing the handwriting of the ordinances that were against us to His Cross. Oh, wondrous work! One might talk thereof by night and day and never weary. View Him rising as our representative, guaranteeing life to us; see Him climbing the skies and casting a largesse of mercies among rebellious men. Consider the influence of His mediatorial authority, the power committed to Him by His Father, for He has power given Him over all flesh that He may give eternal life to as many as the Father gave Him. Listen, listen to His pleading as the Priest upon the throne. What wondrous work is that! Still through the apocalyptic vista gaze; gaze on all the glories of the future when He shall come to reign upon the earth! There you have new fields of light breaking on your ravished view—fresh incentives to wonder, admire, and worship.

And what shall I say of these wondrous works that seem so near and so familiar to our observation and yet baffle our investigation, until the more we scrutinize them the more amazement we feel? The church in the world is kept alive from generation to generation by One whose presence was promised, was bestowed, and is now felt and proved by the saints, the blessed Paraclete, the Comforter whom Jesus sent from the Father. By His agency long seasons of drought and despondency have been ever and anon succeeded by times of refreshing from the presence of the Lord, by revivals and renewals of signs and wonders such as began but did not end in the day of Pentecost. I never know which to wonder at most—God in human flesh, the incarnate Son, or the Holy Spirit dwelling in man. The indwelling is as wonderful as the incarnation. Let every gospel teacher yield up his own soul to the wonder and gratitude that these works of God are fitted to inspire. I like to see the preacher, when he is talking about these things, look like a man wonder struck, gazing forth on a vast expanse, lost in immensity as if he were far out at sea, trembling with adoration as if the chords of his nature vibrated to the mystery and awe that encircle him. There are lovely traces of God's transcendent skill in things minute when peered at through a microscope, but these wondrous works of God are of another order. They display His grander power. Tell not the old, old story as if it had grown trite and trifling in your ears and tripped from off your tongue. Listen to the slow deep mellow voice of the mighty ocean of grace until your soul faints within you. Then speak in tones of strong emotion like those of Paul—"O the depth of the riches both of the wisdom and knowledge of God! how unsearchable are his judgments, and his ways past finding out!"

Yet it becomes you to *speak very plainly*. See how it is put. "I will *talk* of thy wondrous works." Talk is the simplest mode of speech. You cannot all preach, but you can all talk; if some preachers would refrain from rhetoric and tell their plain unvarnished tale, they would succeed better than they do now. Do you think that God meant His ministers to kill themselves in order to come out on Sundays with one or two splendid displays of "intellect" and eloquence? Surely this is not God's way of doing things. I do not believe that Paul ever preached a fine sermon or that Peter ever dreamed of any display of intellect. I asked the other day of one who had heard a sermon if it was likely that sinners would be converted by it. He said, "Oh no, by no means, but it was an intellectual treat." Is there anywhere in the Bible a word about intellectual treats or anything approximating to such an idea? Is there not a country on the other side of the sea where they are attempting fine flashy oratory— sermons that remind you of the way in which they finish up the fireworks; discourses made up of blue lights and blazes? They call it a "peroration," I believe. But the way for the Christian—the real Christian—is to *talk* of God's wondrous works. Tell me the old, old story. Tell it not stalely, but do tell it simply, as to a little child. More glory will come to God from that, more comfort to your soul in reflection, and more benefit to the souls of those you teach, than from all the flights of poetry or the flourishes of rounded periods. They that would win souls must take David's words here and say, "Make me to understand the way of thy precepts," and "I shall talk of thy wondrous works." "Blessed be God," said a farmer at a prayer meeting, "that we were fed last Sunday out of a low crib, for we have mostly had the fodder so high that we poor things could not reach it." When I read that farmer's thanksgiving, I thought it very wise.

When a man is instructed in the faith, he will often speak about these things. Such conversation may be frequent without being irksome. He says, "I will *talk*." Preaching is an exercise to be undertaken now and then, but talking, I believe, is capable of being carried on by some people very nearly every minute of the day. Certainly few persons account it a hardship to talk every day, and when God makes us to understand the way of His precepts, we shall have the Gospel at our fingers' ends so that, whoever we meet with, we shall be able to talk to them in an earnest and simple style about God's salvation. I would, dear friends, that our talk were always seasoned with salt—that our most common conversation were sprinkled with heavenly unction, ministering grace to the hearers.

But though very plain and very frequent, the good psalmist's talk was very much to the point, and it did not lack propriety, for he says, "So shall I talk of thy wondrous works." How does he mean? Why, according to understanding. "Make me to understand, and then I shall talk like an intelligent man." May you, dear brethren and sisters, who do talk about Jesus Christ be enabled to talk about Him in a wise way. Very serious mischief has often come from harping upon some one string. Some men are far more interested in stating their own notions than in unfolding God's counsels. If we understand the way of God's precepts, acquire the language of it, get into the groove of it, then we shall talk with understanding, and there will be a harmony and a wisdom about our utterances that will be blest to the edification of the hearers.

The Prayer of the Student
and the Occupation That Followed

The intimate relation between the prayer of the student and the pursuit he subsequently followed lies partly in the enchantment of this knowledge and the passion to communicate it. A man who understands Christ and His mediatorial work and the Spirit and His sanctifying work cannot be silent. The fire once kindled, the flames will spread. He will be so transported with wonder, admiration, and adoring gratitude at the

great mercy and love of God that it will cause a fermentation within his
breast. He will be like a full vessel wanting vent, and he must have it. As
with a fire in his bones, he will exclaim, "Woe is unto me, if I preach not
the Gospel!" I would to God there were a deeper understanding of the
ways of God, for then many silent tongues must speak. The theme itself
without any remarkable gifts on the part of the man would suffice to secure the attention it strongly claims. As the heart swells with thankfulness, the lips burst forth spontaneously into song. Doubtless Hannah
would tell you that it was easier for a barren wife to restrain her tears
than for a joyful mother to stifle her hymn of praise. Did Jesus love you
when you were all forlorn? Did He find you when a stranger and prove
Himself your friend? Did He shelter you when a sinner and shield you
from all harm? Did He die that you might live? Do you know that Jesus
is your near kinsman and that He takes great delight in redeeming you
for Himself? Let the truth of this but dawn on your heart and, though
your tongue were dumb before, it must now begin to talk.

> Now will I tell to sinners round,
> What a dear Savior I have found,
> I'll point to thy redeeming blood
> And say, "Behold the way to God."

May this stir up some of you who love the Lord and yet never talk
about Him; may it lead you to a holy searching of heart. Surely you have
not such an understanding of Him as you ought to have or else sometimes your silence would be thawed, and your words would betray your
strong emotions.

If I understand the way of God's precepts, then I shall be fully furnished with matter to talk of His wondrous works. What a dreadful thing
it must be for a man to set up to be a teacher of others if he does not
know the things of God experimentally himself. It can be done, you
know, and done very cheaply. You can buy sermons ready lithographed
and guaranteed not to have been preached within so many miles: price
ninepence each. You can be furnished with them for ten shillings and
sixpence a quarter. But there will be a heavy account at the last for the
man who does that sort of thing. It is easy for you to teach in your class
by reading the Sunday School Union notes, getting up the lesson, and
having it all in the head. Ah, but, my dear friend, how will you answer
for having taught children in the Sunday school when you have never
been God's child and never have been taught of God yourself? "Unto the
wicked God saith, What hast thou to do to declare my statutes, or to take
my covenant in thy mouth?" Do not try to teach others what you do not
understand yourself. Go down on your knees and cry, "Make me to understand the way of thy precepts: so shall I talk of thy wondrous works."

Dear brethren, especially you who are to be ministers of the Gospel and have begun to preach, seek a deeper understanding of divine things or else your ministry will be lean and poverty-stricken. Unless you are taken into the confidence of God and initiated into His counsels, you cannot possibly discharge the solemn duties that lie upon the ambassador for Christ. Cry mightily to be well filled with an understanding of the Gospel; so shall you overflow to others and talk of God's wondrous works.

Such sound education will clothe you with authority. A man who, in his own heart, knows what he is talking about and preaches what he has tasted and handled of the good word of grace will put weight into every utterance. It matters but little what language he uses; the power lies not in the garnishing but in the truth itself which he proclaims. It is not the polish of his speech but the fervor of his soul that gives force to his persuasions. Oh, how often my heart has been refreshed by a humble testimony from a poor man who has talked only about what the Lord has done for him. What a power there is about experimental talk. Dry doctrine and pious platitudes borrowed from books fall flat on the ear and pall on the taste, but he who talks of the things that he has made touching the King has a tongue like the pen of a ready writer. I know aged Christians who seem, every time they speak, to drop diamonds and emeralds from their lips; one could wish to treasure up every syllable they utter, not because there is anything very ingenious or original in any sentence, but because there is a sound of abundance of rain in every word, a divine depth, a sacred sweetness, a leaping of life even in each broken utterance that is born on their lips. You say, "That man knows more than he tells. He does not expose all his wares in the window. He has been in the secret place of communion. His face shines though his voice falters." Such teachers may you and I prove in our riper years, having light in ourselves and illuminating all who are within the range of our influence. What God has led us to understand may we be the means of communicating by our ordinary conversation, by speech easy, simple, unostentatious, yet earnest, faithful, and heavenly minded.

Brethren, be up and doing, teaching others what you know. Do not try to teach them what you do not know. As far as you know Christ, speak about Him to your kinsfolk and acquaintance, your friends and neighbors. Our dear brother and elder, the late Mr. Verdon, on such a night as this would have been anxiously looking after any person who seemed to have heard with thankfulness, and he would not have suffered them to leave the place without accosting them in his own gentle manner and beginning to talk to them about Christ. I want some more like him. He has gone home. I pray the Lord that some may be baptized for the dead, to stand in his place and fill up the gap that his removal has made in our ranks. We want a host of wise and prudent Christian talkers. I do not know that we have at present any more urgent need—people who can talk in the train, can talk by the roadside, can talk in the kitchen, can talk in the workshop, can talk across a counter, can, in fact, make opportunities to talk of Jesus. I want you, dear friends, to ask the Lord to qualify you for this service and lead you into it. Some of you appear to be marching backward, for you are even more reticent than you used to be. I would have you like Archimedes when he found out his secret and could not keep it for very joy, but ran down the street crying out, "I have found it! I have found it!" Come, break your guilty silence and cry aloud, "I have found Him of whom Moses in the Law and the Prophets did write, and I cannot help talking about Him."

As for others of you who are not believers, I pray the Lord that you may give a listening ear to the message that I ask others to tell out. Here it is: Jesus Christ came into the world to save sinners. Whosoever believeth in Him hath everlasting life. "He that believeth and is baptized shall be saved." The Lord bring you to accept these tidings, to believe in Jesus, and to find eternal life. Amen.

7

Jesus Interceding for Transgressors

And made intercession for the transgressors (Isaiah 53:12).

Our blessed Lord made intercession for transgressors in so many words while He was being crucified, for He was heard to say, "Father, forgive them; for they know not what they do." It is generally thought that He uttered this prayer at the moment when the nails were piercing His hands and feet and the Roman soldiers were roughly performing their duty as executioners. At the very commencement of His passion He begins to bless His enemies with His prayers. As soon as the rock of our salvation was smitten there flowed forth from it a blessed stream of intercession.

Our Lord fixed His eye upon that point in the character of His persecutors that was most favorable to them, namely, that they knew not what they did. He could not plead their innocence, and therefore He pleaded their ignorance. Ignorance could not excuse their deed, but it did lighten their guilt, and therefore our Lord was quick to mention it as in some measure an extenuating circumstance. The Roman soldiers, of course, knew nothing of His higher mission; they were the mere tools of those who were in power, and though they "mocked him, coming to him, and offering him vinegar," they did so because they misunderstood His claims and regarded Him as a foolish rival of Caesar, only worthy to be ridiculed. No doubt the Savior included these rough Gentiles in His supplication, and perhaps their centurion who glorified God, saying, "Certainly this was a righteous man," was converted in answer to our Lord's prayer. As for the Jews, though they had some measure of light, yet they also acted in the dark. Peter, who would not have flattered any

---

This sermon was taken from *The Metropolitan Tabernacle Pulpit* and was preached on Sunday morning, November 18, 1877.

man, yet said, "And now, brethren, I wot that through ignorance ye did it, as did also your rulers." It is doubtless true that, had they known, they would not have crucified the Lord of Glory, though it is equally clear that they ought to have known Him, for His credentials were clear as noonday. Our Redeemer, in that dying prayer of His, shows how quick He is to see anything that is in any degree favorable to the poor clients whose cause He has undertaken. He spied out in a moment the only fact upon which compassion could find foothold, and He secretly breathed out His loving heart in the cry, "Father, forgive them; for they know not what they do." Our great Advocate will be sure to plead wisely and effi-- ciently on our behalf; He will urge every argument that can be discovered, for His eye, quickened by love, will suffer nothing to pass that may tell in our favor.

The prophet, however, does not, I suppose, intend to confine our thoughts to the one incident that is recorded by the Evangelists, for the intercession of Christ was an essential part of His entire lifework. The mountain's side often heard Him, beneath the chilly night, pouring out His heart in supplications. He might as fitly be called the Man of Prayers as the Man of Sorrows. He was always praying, even when His lips moved not. While He was teaching and working miracles by day, He was silently communing with God and making supplication for men; His nights, instead of being spent in seeking restoration from His exhausting labors, were frequently occupied with intercession. Indeed, our Lord's whole life is a prayer. His career on earth was intercession wrought out in actions. Since, He prayeth best who loveth best, He was a mass of prayer, for He is altogether love. He is not only the channel and the example of prayer, but He is the life and force of prayer. The greatest plea with God is Christ incarnate, Christ fulfilling the law, and Christ bearing the penalty. Jesus Himself is the reasoning and logic of prayer, and He Himself is an ever living prayer to the Most High.

It was part of our Lord's official work to make intercession for the transgressors. He is a priest, and as such He brings His offering and presents prayer on the behalf of the people. Our Lord is the Great High Priest of our profession, and in fulfilling this office we read that He offered up prayers and supplications with strong crying and tears; and we know that He is now offering up prayers for the souls of men. This, indeed, is the great work that He is carrying on today. We rejoice in His finished work and rest in it, but that relates to His atoning sacrifice; His intercession springs out of His atonement, and it will never cease while the blood of His sacrifice retains its power. The blood of sprinkling continues to speak better things than that of Abel. Jesus is pleading now and will be pleading until the heavens shall be no more. For all that come to God by Him He still presents His merits to the Father and pleads the causes of their souls. He urges the grand argument derived from His life and death and so obtains innumerable blessings for the rebellious sons of men.

Admiration for His Grace

I have to direct your attention this morning to our ever-living Lord making intercession for the transgressors, and as I do so I shall pray God, in the first place, that all of us may be roused to admiration for His grace. Come, brethren, gather up your scattered thoughts and meditate upon Him who alone was found fit to stand in the gap and turn away wrath by His pleading. If you will consider His intercession for transgressors, I think you will be struck with the love and tenderness and graciousness of His heart when you recollect that *He offered intercession verbally while He was standing in the midst of their sin.* Sin heard of and sin seen are two very different things. We read of crimes in the newspapers, but we are not at all so horrified as if we had seen them for ourselves. Our Lord actually saw human sin, saw it unfettered and unrestrained, saw it at its worst. Transgressors surrounded His person, and by their sins darted ten thousand arrows into His sacred heart, and yet while they pierced Him, He prayed for them. The mob compassed Him round about, yelling, "Crucify him, crucify him," and His answer was "Father, forgive them"; He knew their cruelty and ingratitude and felt them most keenly but answered them only with a prayer. The great ones of the earth were there, too, sneering and jesting—Pharisee and Sadducee and Herodian—He saw their selfishness, conceit, falsehood, and bloodthirstiness, and yet He prayed. Strong bulls of Bashan had beset Him around, and dogs had compassed Him, yet He interceded for men. Man's sin had stirred up all its strength to slay God's love, and therefore sin had arrived at its worst point, and yet mercy kept pace with malice and outran it, for He sought forgiveness for His tormentors. After killing prophets and other messengers, the wicked murderers were now saying, "This is the Heir: come, let us kill him, that the inheritance may be ours." And yet that heir of all things, who might have called fire from heaven upon them, died crying, "Father, forgive them." He knew that what they did was sin, or He would not have prayed "forgive them," yet He set their deed in the least unfavorable light and said, "they know not what they do." He set His own sonship to work on their behalf and appealed to His Father's love to pardon them for His sake. Never was virtue set in so fair a frame before, never goodness came so adorned with abundant love as in the person of the Lord Jesus, yet they hated Him all the more for His loveliness and gathered around Him with the deeper spite because of His infinite goodness. He saw it all and felt the sin as you and I cannot feel it, for His heart was purer and therefore more tender than ours; He saw that the tendency of sin was to put Him to death and all like Him, yes and to slay God Himself if it could achieve its purpose, for man had become a deicide and must needs crucify his God—and yet, though His holy soul saw and loathed all this tendency and atrocity of transgression, He still made intercession for the transgressors. I do not know whether I convey my own idea, but to me it seems beyond measure wonderful that He should know sin so thoroughly, understand its heinousness, and see the drift of it and feel it so wantonly assailing Himself when He was doing nothing but deeds of kindness; yet with all that vivid sense of the vileness of sin upon Him, even there and then He made intercession for the transgressors, saying, "Father, forgive them; for they know not what they do."

Another point of His graciousness was also clear on that occasion, namely, that He should *thus intercede while in agony.* It is marvelous that He should be able to call His mind away from His own pains to consider their transgressions. You and I, if we are subject to great pains of body, do not find it easy to command our minds and especially to collect our thoughts and restrain them so as to forgive the person inflicting the pain and even to invoke blessings on his head. Remember that your Lord was suffering while He made intercession, beginning to suffer the pangs of death, suffering in soul as well as in body, for He had freshly come from the Garden, where His soul was exceeding sorrowful, even to death. Yet in the midst of that depression of spirit, which might well have made Him forgetful of the wretched beings who were putting Him to death, He forgets Himself, and He only thinks of them and pleads for them. I am sure that we should have been taken up with our pains even if we had not been moved to some measure of resentment against our tormentors, but we hear no complaints from our Lord, no accusations lodged with God, no angry replies to them, such as Paul once gave— "God shall smite thee, thou whited wall," not even a word mourning or complaining concerning the indignities that He endured, but His dear heart all ascended to heaven in that one blessed petition for His enemies, which there and then He presented to His Father.

But I will not confine your thoughts to that incident because, as I have already said, the prophet's words had a wider range. To me it is marvelous *that He, being pure, should plead for transgressors at all*— for you and for me among them—let the wonder begin there. Sinners by nature, sinners by practice, willful sinners, sinners who cling to sin with a terrible tenacity, sinners who come back to sin after we have smarted for it, yet the Just One has espoused our cause and has become a suitor for our pardon. We are sinners who omit duties when they are pleasures, who follow after sins that are known to involve sorrow, sinners, therefore, of the most foolish kind, wanton, willful sinners, and yet He who hates sin has deigned to take our part and plead the causes of our souls. Our Lord's hatred of sin is as great as His love to sinners; His indignation against everything impure is as great as that of the thrice holy God who revenges and is furious when He comes into contact with evil; yet this divine Prince, of whom we sing, "Thou lovest righteousness and hatest wickedness," espouses the cause of transgressors and pleads for them. Oh, matchless grace! Surely angels wonder at this stretch of condescending love. Brethren, words fail me to speak of it. I ask you to adore!

Further, it is to me a very wonderful fact that *in His glory He should still be pleading for sinners.* There are some men who when they have reached to high positions forget their former associates. They knew the poor and needy friend once, for, as the proverb has it, poverty brings us strange bedfellows, but when they have risen out of such conditions, they are ashamed of the people whom once they knew. Our Lord is not thus forgetful of the degraded clients whose cause He espoused in the days of His humiliation. Yet, though I know his constancy, I marvel and admire. The Son of Man on earth pleading for sinners is very gracious, but I am overwhelmed when I think of His interceding for sinners now that He reigns yonder, where harps unnumbered tune His praise and cherubim and seraphim count it their glory to be less than nothing at His feet, where all the glory of His Father is resplendent in Him, and He sits at the right hand of God in divine favor and majesty unspeakable. How can we hear without amazement that the King of Kings and Lord of Lords occupies Himself with caring for transgressors—caring indeed for you and me. It is condescension that He should commune with the bloodwashed before His throne and allow the perfect spirits to be His companions, but that His heart should steal away from all heaven's felicities to remember such poor creatures as we are and to make incessant prayer on our behalf, this is like His own loving self—it is Christlike, Godlike. I think I see at this moment our great High Priest pleading before the throne, wearing His jeweled breastplate and His garments of glory and beauty, wearing our names upon His breast and His shoulders in the most holy place. What a vision of incomparable love! It is a fact and no mere dream. He is within the Holy of Holies, presenting the one sacrifice. His prayers are always heard and heard for us, but the marvel is that the Son of God should condescend to exercise such an office and make intercession for transgressors. This matchless grace well nigh seals my lips, but it opens the floodgates of my soul, and I would fain pause to worship Him whom my words fail to set forth.

Again, it is gloriously gracious *that our Lord should continue to do this*; for lo, these eighteen hundred years and more He has gone into His glory, yet has He never ceased to make intercession for transgressors. Never on heaven's most joyous holiday when all His armies are marshaled, and in their glittering squadrons pass in review before the King of Kings has He forgotten His redeemed ones. The splendors of heaven have not made Him indifferent to the sorrows of earth. Never, though, for aught we know, He may have created myriads of worlds, and though assuredly He has been ruling the courses of the entire universe, never once, I say, has He suspended His incessant pleading for the transgressors. Nor will He, for the Holy Scriptures lead us to believe that as long as He lives as mediator, He will intercede. He is able to save them to the uttermost that come to God by Him, seeing He ever lives to make intercession for them. He lived and lives to intercede, as if this were the express object of His living. Beloved, as long as the great Redeemer lives and there is a sinner still to come to Him, He will still continue to intercede. Oh, my Master, how shall I praise You? Had You undertaken such an office now and then and had You gone into the royal presence once in a while to intercede for some special cases, it would have been divinely gracious on Your part, but that You should always be a suppliant and never cease to intercede surpasses all our praise. Wonderful are His words as written in prophecy by Isaiah—"For Zion's sake will I not hold my peace, and for Jerusalem's sake I will not rest, until the righteousness thereof go forth as brightness, and the salvation thereof as a lamp that burneth." As the lamp in the temple went not out, so neither has our Advocate ceased to plead day nor night. Unwearied in His labor of love, without a pause He has urged our suit before the Father's face. Beloved, I will not enlarge, I cannot, for adoration of such love quite masters me, but let your hearts be enlarged with abounding love to such an intercessor as this, who made, who does make, and who always will make intercession for the transgressors.

I have said, "will make," and indeed this is no bare assertion of mine, for my text may be read in the future as well as in the past. Indeed, as you will perceive upon a little thought, it must have been meant to be understood in the future since the prophecy was written some seven hundred years before our Lord had breathed His intercessory prayer at the cross. Although the prophet, in order to make his language pictorial and vivid, puts it in the past tense, it was actually in the future to him, and therefore we cannot err in reading it in the future, as I have done—"he *shall* make intercession for the transgressors." Constant love puts up a ceaseless plea. Endless compassion breathes its endless prayer. Until the last of the redeemed has been gathered home, that interceding breath shall never stay, nor cease to prevail.

Confidence in Him

Thus have I called you to feel admiration for His grace, and now, secondly, I do earnestly pray that we may be led of the Holy Spirit so to view His intercession for transgressors as to put our confidence in Him. There is ground for a sinner's confidence in Christ, and there is abundant argument for the believer's complete reliance in Him from the fact of His perpetual intercession.

Let me show you this first, because, beloved, *His intercession succeeds.* God hears Him, of that we do not doubt, but what is the basis of His intercession? For whatever that is, seeing it makes the intercession to be successful, we may safely rest on it. Read carefully the verse: "Because he hath poured out his soul unto death: and he was numbered with the transgressors; and he bare the sin of many." See, then, the success of His plea arises out of His substitution. He pleads and prevails because He has borne the sin of those for whom He intercedes. The mainstay and strength of His prevalence in His intercession lies in the completeness of the sacrifice that He offered when He bore the sin of many. Come, then, my soul, if Christ's prayer prevails because of this, so will your faith. Resting on the same foundation, your faith will be equally secure of acceptance. Come, my heart, rest on that truth—"he bare the sin of many." Throw yourself with all your sin upon His substitution and feel that this is a safe resting place for your believing, because it is a solid basis for your Lord's intercession. The perfect sacrifice will bear all the strain that can possibly come upon it; test it by the strongest faith and see for yourself; plead it with the boldest requests and learn its boundless prevalence. You may urge the plea of the precious blood with the Father, seeing the Lord Jesus has urged it and has never failed.

Now, again, *there is reason for transgressors to come and trust in Jesus Christ, seeing He pleads for them.* You need never be afraid that Christ will cast you out when you can hear Him pleading for you. If a son had been disobedient and had left his father's house and were to come back again, if he had any fear about his father's receiving him, it would all disappear if he stood listening at the door and heard his father praying for him. "Oh," says he, "my coming back is an answer to my father's prayer, he will gladly enough receive me." Whenever a soul comes to Christ it need have no hesitancy, seeing Christ has already prayed for it that it might be saved. I tell you, transgressors, Christ prays for you when you do not pray for yourselves. Did He not say of His believing people, "Neither pray I for these alone, but for them also which shall believe on me through their word"? Before His elect become believers they have a place in His supplications. Before you know yourselves to be transgressors and have any desire for pardon, while as yet you are lying dead in sin, His intercession has gone up even for such as you are. "Father, forgive them" was a prayer for those who had never sought forgiveness for themselves. And when you dare not pray for yourselves, He is still praying for you. When under a sense of sin you dare not lift so much as your eyes toward heaven, when you think "Surely it would be in vain for me to seek my heavenly Father's face," He is pleading for you. Aye, and when you cannot plead, when through deep distress of mind you feel choked in the very attempt to pray, when the language of supplication seems to blister your lip because you feel yourself to be so unworthy, when you cannot force even a holy groan from your despairing heart, He still pleads for you. Oh, what encouragement this ought to give you. If you cannot pray, He can, and if you feel as if your prayers must be shut out, yet His intercession cannot be denied. Come and trust Him! Come and trust Him! He who pleads for you will not reject you; do not entertain so unkind a thought, but come and cast yourself upon Him. Has He not said, "Him that cometh to me I will in no wise cast out"? Venture upon the assured truth of that word, and you will be received into the abode of His love.

I am sure too that if Jesus Christ pleads for transgressors as transgressors, while as yet they have not begun to pray for themselves, He will be sure to hear them when they are at last led to pray. When the transgressor becomes a penitent, when he weeps because he has gone astray, let us be quite sure that the Lord of mercy who went after him in his sin will come to meet him now that he returns. There can be no doubt about that. I have known what it is to catch at this text when I have been heavy in heart. I have seen my sinfulness, and I have been filled with distress, but I have blessed the Lord Jesus Christ that He makes intercession for the transgressors, for then I may venture to believe that He intercedes for me, since I am a transgressor beyond all doubt. Then again, when my spirit has revived, and I have said, "But I am a child of God, and I know I am born from above," then I have drawn a further inference—if He makes intercession for transgressors, then depend upon it, He is even more intent upon pleading for His own people. If He is heard for those who are out of the way, assuredly He will be heard for those who have returned to the shepherd and bishop of their souls. For them above all others He will be sure to plead, for He lives to intercede for all who come to God by Him.

In order that our confidence may be increased, *consider the effect of our Lord's intercession for transgressors*. Remember, first, that many of the worst of transgressors have been *preserved in life* in answer to Christ's prayer. Had it not been for His pleading, they would have been dead long ago. You know the parable of the fig tree that cumbered the ground, bearing no fruit, and impoverishing the soil. The master of the vineyard said, "Cut it down," but the vinedresser said, "Let it alone this year also, till I shall dig about it, and dung it: and if it bear fruit, well." Need I say who He is that stays the ax that else had long ago been laid at the root of the barren tree? I tell you, ungodly men and women, that you owe your very lives to my Lord's interference on your behalf. You did not hear the intercession, but the Great Owner of the vineyard heard it, and in answer to the gracious entreaties of His Son He has let you live a little longer. Still, are you where the Gospel can come at you and where the Holy Spirit can renew you? Is there no ground for faith in this gracious fact? Can you not trust in Him through whose instrumentality you are yet alive? Say to your heavenly Father,

> Lord, and am I yet alive,
> Not in torments, not in hell!
> Still doth thy good Spirit strive—
> With the chief of sinners dwell?

And then believe in Him to whose pleading you owe the fact that you are within reach of mercy. Well does it become you to confide in Him who has already been your preserver from death and hell. May the divine Spirit teach you the reasonableness of my argument and lead you at once to humble faith in Jesus.

Remember, next, that *the gift of the Holy Spirit* which is needful for the quickening of transgressors was the result of Christ's intercession. Our poet was right when he said—

> 'Tis by thine interceding breath
> The Spirit dwells with men.

I do not doubt but that between the prayer of Christ for His murderers and the outpouring of the Holy Spirit at Pentecost there was an intimate connection. As the prayer of Stephen brought Saul into the church and made him an apostle, so the prayer of Christ brought in three thousand at Pentecost to become His disciples. The Spirit of God was given "to the rebellious also" in answer to the pleadings of our Lord. Now, it is a great blessing thus to have the Spirit of God given to the sons of men, and if this comes through Jesus' prayers, let us trust in Him, for what will not come if we rely upon His power? Upon sinners He will still display His power; they will be pricked in their hearts and will believe in Him whom they have pierced.

It is through Christ's intercession that *our poor prayers are accepted with God*. John, in the Revelation, saw another angel standing at the altar, having a golden censor, to whom there was given much incense, that he should offer it with the prayers of all saints upon the golden altar that was before the throne. Whence comes the much incense? What is it but Jesus' merits? Our prayers are only accepted because of His prayers. If, then, the intercession of Christ for transgressors has made the prayers of transgressors to be accepted, let us without wavering put our trust in

Him, and let us show it by offering our supplications with a full assurance of faith and an unstaggering confidence in the promise of our covenant God. Are not all the promises yes and amen in Christ Jesus? Let us remember Him and ask in faith, nothing wavering.

It is through the prayers of Christ, too, that we are *kept in the hour of temptation*. Remember what He said to Peter, "I have prayed for thee, that thy faith fail not," when Satan desired to have him and sift him as wheat. "Father, keep them from the evil" is a part of our Lord's supplication, and His Father hears Him always. Well, if we are kept in the midst of temptation from being destroyed because Christ pleads for us, let us never fear to trust ourselves in His kind, careful hands. He can keep us, for He has kept us. If His prayers have delivered us out of the hand of Satan, His eternal power can bring us safely home, though death lies in the way.

Indeed, it is because He pleads *that we are saved at all*. He is able also to save them to the uttermost that come to God by Him, seeing He ever lives to make intercession for them. This, also, is one grand reason why we are able to challenge all the accusations of the world and of the Devil, for "Who is he that condemneth? It is Christ that died, yea rather, that is risen again, who is even at the right hand of God, who also maketh intercession for us." Satan's charges are all answered by our Advocate. He defends us at the judgment seat when we stand there, like Joshua, in filthy garments, accused of the Devil; therefore the verdict is always given in our favor—"Take away the filthy garments from him." Oh, you that would bring slanderous accusations against the saints of God, they will not damage us in the court of the great King, for "if any man sin, we have an advocate with the Father, Jesus Christ the righteous." Think, my dear brethren and sisters, of what the intercession of Jesus has done, and you will clearly perceive great inducements to place your sole reliance in your Lord. You who have never trusted Him, will you not this very morning begin to do so? Come, weary heart, take the Lord Jesus to be your confidence—what more do you want? Can you desire a better friend than He is, a more prevalent advocate before the throne? Come, leave all other trusts and yield yourselves to Him this morning. I pray you accept this advice of love. And you, you saints, if you are foolish enough to have doubts and fears, come, see how Jesus pleads for you. Give Him your burden to bear, leave with Him your anxieties at this moment that He may care for you. He will carry on your suit before the eternal throne and carry it through to success. He who engages a solicitor to manage his legal business among men leaves his affairs in his hands, and he who has such a pleader before God as Christ Jesus, the Wonderful, Counselor, has no need to torment himself with anxieties. Rather let him rest in Jesus and wait the result with patience.

> Give him, my soul, thy cause to plead,
> Nor doubt the Father's grace.

So much, then, for the duty of exercising confidence in Him. May the Holy Spirit fill you with faith and peace.

Obedience to His Example

And now, in the third place, I pray that our text may inspire us with the spirit of obedience to His example. I say obedience to His example, for I take the example of Christ to be an embodied precept as much binding upon us as His written commands. The life of Christ is a precept to those who profess to be His disciples. Now, brethren in Christ, may I put a few practical matters before you, and will you endeavor by the help of God's Spirit to carry them out?

First, then, your Lord makes intercession for the transgressors, therefore *imitate Him by forgiving all transgressions against yourself.* Have any offended you? Let the very recollection of the offense as far as possible pass from your minds, for none have ever injured you as men injured Him—let me say, as you yourself have injured Him. They have not nailed you to a cross nor pierced your hands and feet and side; if *He* said, "Father, forgive them," well may you say the same. Ten thousand talents did you owe? Yet He forgave you all that debt, not without a grievous outlay to Himself. Your brother owes you but a hundred pence, will you take him by the throat? Will you not rather freely forgive him even to seventy times seven? Can you not forgive him? If you find it to be impossible, I will not speak to you any longer as a Christian, because I must doubt if you are a believer at all. The Lord cannot accept you while you are unforgiving, since He Himself says, "Therefore if thou bring thy gift to the altar, and there rememberest that thy brother hath ought against thee; leave there thy gift before the altar, and go thy way; first be reconciled to thy brother, and then come and offer thy gift." If peace be not made, you will not be accepted. God hears not those in whose hearts malice and enmity find a lodging. Yet I would speak to you in tones of love rather than with words of threatening; as a follower of the gentle Christ I beseech you imitate Him in this, and you shall find rest and comfort to your own soul. From the day in which Christ forgives you, rise to that nobility of character that finds a pleasure in forgiving all offenses fully and frankly for Christ's sake. Surely, the atonement that He offered, if it satisfied God, may well satisfy you and make amends for the sin of your brother against you as well as against the Lord. Jesus took upon Himself the transgressions of the second table of the law as well as of the first, and will you bring a suit against your brother for the sin that Jesus bore? Brethren, you must forgive, for the blood has blotted the record! Let these words of Scripture drop upon your hearts like gentle dew from heaven—"Be ye kind one to another, tenderhearted, forgiving one another, even as God for Christ's sake hath forgiven you."

Next, imitate Christ, dear friends, *in pleading for yourselves*. Since you are transgressors and you see that Jesus intercedes for transgressors, make bold to say, "If He pleads for such as I am, I will put in my humble petition and hope to be heard through Him. Since I hear Him cry, 'Father, forgive them,' I will humbly weep at His feet and try to mingle my faint and trembling plea with His all-prevalent supplication." When Jesus says, "Father, forgive them," it will be your wisdom to cry, "Father, forgive *me*." Dear hearer, that is the way to be saved. Let your prayers hang, like the golden bells, upon the skirts of the great High Priest; He will carry them within the veil and make them ring out sweetly there. As music borne on the breeze is heard afar, so shall your prayers have a listener in heaven because Jesus wafts them there. Since your prayers are feeble, yoke them to the omnipotence of His intercession; let His merits be as wings on which they may soar and His power as hands with which they may grasp the priceless boons. What shall I say to those who refuse to pray when they have such an encouragement as the aid of Jesus? Tones of tenderness are suitable when addressing the ungodly, when we would persuade them to pray; if they refuse the intercession of Jesus Christ Himself, then must we add our solemn warnings. If you perish, your blood be on your own heads; we must say Amen to your condemnation and bear witness that you deserve to be doubly punished. Rejecters of great mercy must expect great wrath. The intercession of your Savior, when refused, will be visited upon you most terribly in the day when He becomes your judge.

Let us imitate our Lord in a third point, dear friends; namely, if we have been forgiven our transgressions, *let us now intercede for transgressors*, since Jesus does so. He is the great example to all His disciples, and, if He makes it His constant business to supplicate for sinners, should not His people unite with Him? Therefore would I stir up your pure minds by way of remembrance to come together in your hundreds and in your thousands to pray. Never let your prayer meetings decline. Let us, as a church, make intercession for transgressors and never rest from seeking the conversion of all around us. I trust that every day, so often as you bow the knee for yourselves, you will make intercession for the transgressors. Poor things, many of them are sinning against their own souls, but they know not what they do. They think to find pleasure in sin; in this also they know not what they do. They break the Sabbath, they despise the sanctuary, they reject Christ, they go downward to hell with mirth, singing merry glees as if they were going to a wedding feast;

they know not what they do. But you do know what they are doing. By
your humanity—scarcely shall I need to urge a stronger motive—I say,
by mere humanity, I beseech you, do all you can for these poor souls,
and especially pray for them. It is not much you are asked to do; you are
not pointed to the Cross and bidden to bleed there for sinners, you are
but asked to make intercession. Intercession is an honorable service; it is
an ennobling thing that a sinner like you should be allowed to entreat the
King for others. If you could have permission to frequent the queen's
courts, you would not think it a hardship to be asked to present a petition
for another; it would be to you a delight to be enjoyed, a privilege to be
snatched at eagerly, that you should be permitted to present requests for
others. Oh, stand where Abraham stood and plead for sinners; Sodom
could scarce be worse than many portions of the world at this hour.
Plead, then, with all your hearts. Plead again and again and again with
the Lord, though you be but dust and ashes, and cease not until the Lord
say, "I have heard the petition, I will bless the city, I will save the millions, and my Son shall be glorified."

I have not quite done, for I have a further duty to speak of, and it is
this: let us take care, dear friends, that if we do plead for others, *we mix
with it the doing of good to them*, because it is not recorded that He
made intercession for transgressors until it is first written, "he bare the
sin of many." For us to pray for sinners without instructing them, without exerting ourselves to arouse them or making any sacrifice for their
conversion, without using any likely means for their impression and
conviction would be a piece of mere formality on our part. According to
our ability we must prove the sincerity of our petitions by our actions.
Prayer without effort is falsehood, and that cannot be pleasing to God.
Yield up yourselves to seek the good of others, and then may you intercede with honest hearts.

Lastly, *if Christ appears in heaven for us, let us be glad to appear on
earth for Him.* He owns us before God and the holy angels, let us not be
ashamed to confess Him before men and devils. If Christ pleads with
God for men, let us not be backward to plead with men for God. If He
by His intercession saves us to the uttermost, let us hasten to serve Him
to the uttermost. If He spends eternity in intercession for us, let us spend
our time in intercession for His cause. If He thinks of us, we ought also
to think of His people, and especially supplicate for His afflicted. If He
watches our cases and adapts His prayers to our necessities, let us observe the needs of His people and plead for them with understanding.
Alas, how soon do men weary of pleading with our Lord. If a whole day
is set apart for prayer and the meeting is not carefully managed, it readily becomes a weariness of the flesh. Prayer meetings very easily lose
their flame and burn low. Shame on these laggard spirits and this heavy

flesh of ours, which needs to be pampered with liveliness and brevity or we go to sleep at our devotions. Forever is not too long for Him to plead, and yet an hour tries us here. On and on, and on through all the ages, still His intercession rises to the throne; yet we flag and our prayers are half dead in a short season. See, Moses lets his hands hang down, and Amelek is defeating Joshua in the plain! Can we endure to be thus losing victories and causing the Enemy to triumph? If your ministers are unsuccessful, if your laborers for Christ in foreign lands make little headway, if the work of Christ drags, is it not because in the secret place of intercession we have but little strength? The restraining of prayer is the weakening of the church. If we aroused ourselves to lay hold upon the covenant angel and resolutely cried, "I will not let thee go, except thou bless me," we should enrich ourselves and our age. If we used more of the strong reasons which make up the weapon of all prayer, our victories would not be so few and far between. Our interceding Lord is hindered for lack of an interceding church; the kingdom comes not because so little use is made of the throne of grace. Get to your knees, my children, for on your knees you conquer. Go to the mercy seat and remain there. What better argument can I use with you than this—Jesus is there, and if you desire His company, you must oftentimes resort thither? If you want to taste His dearest, sweetest love, do what He is doing; union of work will create a new communion of heart. Let us never be absent when praying men meet together. Let us make a point of frequenting assemblies gathered for prayer, even if we give up other occupations. While we live, let us be above all things men of prayer, and when we die, if nothing else can be said of us, may men give us this epitaph, which is also our Lord's memorial—"He made intercession for the transgressors." Amen.

8

Daniel: A Pattern for Pleaders

O Lord, hear; O Lord, forgive; O Lord, hearken and do; defer not, for thine own sake, O my God: for thy city and thy people are called by thy name (Daniel 9:19).

Daniel was a man in very high position in life. It is true he was not living in his own native land, but, in the providence of God, he had been raised to great eminence under the dominion of the country in which he dwelt. He might, therefore, naturally have forgotten his poor kinsmen; many have done so. Alas! we have known some that have even forgotten their poor fellow Christians when they have grown in grace and have thought themselves too good to worship with the poorer sort when they themselves have grown rich in this world's goods. But it was not so with Daniel. Though he had been made a president of the empire, yet he was still a Jew; he felt himself still one with the seed of Israel. In all the afflictions of his people he was afflicted, and he felt it his honor to be numbered with them, and his duty and his privilege to share with them all the bitterness of their lot. If he could not become despised and as poor as they, if God's providence had made him to be distinguished, yet his heart would make no distinction; he would remember them and pray for them and would plead that their desolation might yet be removed.

Daniel was also a man very high in spiritual things. Is he not one of God's three mighties in the Old Testament? He is mentioned with two others in a celebrated verse as being one of three whose intercessions God would have heard if He had heard any intercessions. But though thus full of grace himself (and for that very reason), he

This sermon was taken from *The Metropolitan Tabernacle Pulpit* and was preached on Sunday evening, September 25, 1870.

stooped to those who were in a low state. Rejoicing as he did before God as to his own lot, he sorrowed and cried by reason of those from whom joy was banished. It is a sad fault with those Christians who think themselves full of grace when they begin to despise their fellows. They may rest assured they are greatly mistaken in the estimate they have formed of themselves. But it is a good sign when your own heart is fruitful and healthy before God, when you do condescend to those that backslide and search after such as are weak and bring again such as were driven away. When you have, like your Master, a tender sympathy for others, then are you rich in divine things. Daniel showed his intimate sympathy with his poorer and less gracious brethren in the way of prayer. He would have shown that sympathy in other ways had occasions occurred, and no doubt he did, but this time the most fitting way of proving his oneness with them was in becoming an intercessor for them.

My object here and now will be to stir up the people of God, and especially the members of this church, to abound exceedingly in prayer, more and more to plead with God for the prosperity of His church and the extension of the Redeemer's kingdom.

First, our text gives us *a model of prayer*; and secondly, *it and its surroundings give us encouragement for prayer*.

A Model of Prayer

I think I may notice this first as to the antecedents of the prayer. This prayer of Daniel *was not offered without consideration*. He did not come to pray as some people do, as though it were a thing that required no forethought whatever. We are constantly told we ought to prepare our sermons, and I surely think that if a man does not prepare his sermons he is very blameworthy. But are we never to prepare when we speak to God, and only when we speak to man? Is there to be no preparation of the heart of man for God when we open our mouths before the Lord? Do not you think we often do, both in private and public, begin to pray without any kind of consideration, and the words come, and then we try to quicken the words, rather than the desires coming, and the words coming like garments to clothe them withal?

But Daniel's considerations lay in this first, *he studied the books*. He had with him an old manuscript of the prophet Jeremiah. He read that through. Perceiving such and such things spoken of, he prayed for them. Perceiving such and such a time given, and knowing that that time was almost come, he prayed the more earnestly. Oh! that you studied your Bibles more! Oh! that we all did! How we could plead the promises! How often we should prevail with God when we could hold Him to His Word, and say, "Fulfill this word to Your servant, whereon You have caused me to hope." Oh! it is grand praying when our mouths are full of God's Word, for there is no word that can prevail with Him like His own. You tell a man, when you ask him for such and such a thing, "You yourself said you would do so and so." You have him then. And so when you can lay hold on the covenant promises with this consecrated grip, "You have said! you have said!" then have you every opportunity of prevailing with Him. May our prayers then spring out of our scriptural studies; may our acquaintance with the Word be such that we shall be qualified to pray a Daniel prayer.

He had, moreover, it is clear if you read the prayer again, studied the history of his people. He gives a little outline of it from the day in which they came out of Egypt. Christian people should be acquainted with the history of the church—if not with the church of the past, certainly with the church of today. We make ourselves acquainted with the position of the Prussian army, and we will buy new maps about once a week to see all the places and the towns. Should not Christians make themselves acquainted with the position of Christ's army and revise their maps to see how the kingdom of God is progressing in England, in the United States, on the Continent, or in the mission stations throughout the world? All our prayers would be much better if we knew more about the church and especially about our own church. I am afraid I must say it—I am afraid there are some members of the church that do not know what the church is doing—hardly know what is meant by some of our enterprises. Brethren, know well the church's needs as far as you can ascertain them, and then, like Daniel's, your prayer will be a prayer founded upon information; with the promises of God and the fact of the church's wants, you will pray prayers of the spirit and of the understanding. Let that stand for earnest consideration.

But next, Daniel's prayer was *mingled with much humiliation.* According to the Oriental custom which expresses the inward thought and feeling by the outward act, he put on a coarse garment made of black hair called sackcloth; then taking handfuls of ashes, he cast them on his head and over the cloth that covered him and then he knelt down in the very dust in secret. These outward symbols were made to express the humiliation which he felt before God. We always pray best when we pray out of the depths; when the soul gets low enough, she gets a leverage, she can then plead with God. I do not say we ought to ask to see all the evil of our own hearts. One good man prayed that prayer very often. He is mentioned in some of the Puritan writers, a minister of the Gospel. It pleased God to hear his prayer, and he never rejoiced afterward. It was with great difficulty that he was even kept from suicide, so deep and dreadful was the agony he experienced when he did begin to see his sin as he wanted to see it. It is best to see as much of that as God would have us see of it. You cannot see too much of Christ, but you might see even too much of your sin. Yet, brethren, this is rarely the case. We need to see much our deep needs, our great sins, for ah! that prayer shall go highest that comes from the lowest. To stoop well is a grand art in prayer. To pour out the last drop of anything like self-righteousness, to be able to say from the very heart, "Not for our righteousness' sake do we plead with thee, O God, for we have sinned, and our fathers too." Put the negative, the weightiest negative, upon any idea of pleading human merit. When you can do this, then are you in the right way to pray a prayer that will move the arm of God and bring you down a blessing. Oh, some of you ungodly ones have tried to pray, but you have not bowed yourselves. Proud prayers may knock their heads on mercy's lintel, but they can never pass through the portal. You cannot expect anything of God unless you put yourself in the right place, that is, as a beggar at His footstool; then will He hear you, and not until then.

Daniel's prayer instructs us in the next point. *It was excited by zeal for God's glory*. We may sometimes pray with wrong motives. If I seek the conversion of souls in my ministry, is not that a good motive? Yes, it is; but suppose I desire the conversion of souls in order that people may say, "What a useful minister he is," that is a bad motive, which spoils it all. If I am a member of a Christian church, and I pray for its prosperity, is not that right? Certainly; but if I desire its prosperity merely that I and others may be able to say, "See our zeal for the Lord! See how God blesses us rather than others!" that is a wrong motive. The motive is this, "Oh, that God could be glorified that Jesus might see the reward of His sufferings! Oh! that sinners might be saved so that God might have new tongues to praise Him, new hearts to love Him! Oh! that sin were put an end to, that the holiness, righteousness, mercy, and power of God might be magnified!" This is the way to pray; when your prayers seek God's glory, it is God's glory to answer your prayers. When you are sure that God is in the case, you are on a good footing. If you are praying for that which will greatly glorify Him, you may rest assured your prayer will speed. But if it does not speed and it be not for His glory, why, then you may be better content to be without it than with it. So pray, but keep your bowstring right; it will be unfit to shoot the arrow of prayer unless this be your bowstring, "God's glory, God's glory"—this above all, first, last, and midst, the one object of my prayer.

Then coming closer to the prayer, I would have you notice *how intense Daniel's prayer was*. "O Lord, hear: O Lord, forgive: O Lord, hearken and do, defer not for thine own sake." The very repetitions here express vehemence. It is a great fault of some people in public prayer when they repeat the name, "O Lord, O Lord, O Lord," so often—it often amounts to taking God's name in vain and is, indeed, a vain repetition. But when the reiteration of that sacred name comes out of the soul, then it is no vain repetition; then it cannot be repeated too often and is not open to anything like the criticism that I used just now. So you will notice how the prophet here seems to pour out his soul with "O Lord, O Lord, O Lord," as if, if the first knock at mercy's door does not open it, he will knock again and make the gate to shake and then the third time come with another thundering stroke if, perhaps, he may succeed. Cold prayers ask God to deny them; only importunate prayers will be replied to. When the church of God cannot take no for an answer, she shall not have no for an answer. When a pleading soul *must* have it, when the Spirit of God works mightily in him so that he cannot let the angel go without a blessing, the angel shall not go until he has given the blessing to such a pleading one. Brethren, if there be only one among us that can pray as Daniel did, with intensity, the blessing will come. Let this encourage any earnest man or woman here that fears that others are not excited to prayer as they should be. Dear brother, do you undertake it? Dear sister, in God's name, do you undertake it? God will send a blessing to many through the prayer of one. But how much better would it be if many a score of men here, aye, the entire church of God, were stirred up to this, that we give Him no rest until He establish and make Jerusalem a praise in the earth! Oh! that our prayers could get beyond praying until they got to agonizing. As soon as Zion travailed—you know that word—as soon as she *travailed* she brought forth children. Not until it comes to travail—not until then—may we expect to see much done. God send such travailing to each one of us, and then the promise is near to fulfilling

But coming still to the text, and a little more closely, I want to observe that this remarkable prayer was *a prayer of understanding* as well as earnestness; some people in their earnestness talk nonsense, and I think I have heard prayers that God might understand, but I am sure I did not. Now here is a prayer that we can understand as well as God. It begins thus, "O Lord, hear." He asks an audience. This is how the petitioner does if he comes before an earthly majesty: he asks to be heard. He begins with that, O Lord, hear. "I am not worthy to be heard; if you shut me and my case out of hearing, it will be just." He asks an audience, he gets it, and now he goes at once to his point without delay, "O Lord, forgive." He knows what he wants. Sin was the mischief, the cause of all the suffering. He puts his hand on it. Oh! it is grand when one knows what one is praying for. Many prayers maunder and wander—the praying person evidently thinks he is doing a good thing in saying certain good phrases, but the prayer that hits the target in the center is the prayer it is good to pray. God teach us to pray so. "O Lord, forgive."

Then observe how he presses the point home. "O Lord, hearken and do." If You have forgiven—he does not stop a minute, but here comes another prayer quick on the heels of it. Do, good Lord, interpose for the rebuilding of Jerusalem—do interpose for the redemption of Your captive people; do interpose for the reestablishment of sacred worship. It is well when our prayers can fly fast, one after another, as we feel we are gaining ground. You know in wrestling (and that is a model of prayer) much depends on the foothold, but oftentimes there is much depending upon swiftness and celerity of action. So in prayer. "Hear, me, my Lord! You have heard me, forgive me. Have I come so far, then work for me—work the blessings I want." Follow up your advantage; build another prayer on the answer that you have. If you have received a great blessing, say, "*Because* He has inclined His ear to me, therefore will I call upon Him; because He has heard me once, therefore will I call again." Such a prayer proves the thoughtfulness of him who prays. It is a prayer offered in the spirit, and with understanding also.

And now one other thing. The prayer of Daniel was *a prayer of holy nearness.* You catch that thought in the expression, "O *my* God." Ah! we pray at a distance oftentimes; we pray to God as if we were slaves lying at His throne-foot; as if we might, perhaps, be heard, but we did not know. But when God helps us to pray as we should we come right to Him, even to His feet, and we say, "Hear me, O my God." He is God; therefore, we must be reverent. He is my God; therefore, we may be familiar; we may come close to Him. I believe some of the expressions that Martin Luther used in prayer, if I were to use them, would be little short of blasphemy, but as Martin Luther used them I believe they were deeply devout and acceptable with God, because he knew how to come close to God. You know how your little child climbs your knee; he gives you a kiss, and he will say to you many little things that if a person in the market were to say, you could not bear; they must not be said. No other being may be so familiar with you as your child. But oh! a child of God—when his heart is right—how near he gets to his God; he pours out his childlike complaint in childlike language before the Most High. Brethren, this is to be noted well, that though he is thus pleading and in the position of humility, yet still he is not in the position of slavery. It is still "O *my God*"—he grasps the covenant; faith perceives the relationship to be unbroken between the soul and God and pleads that relation: "O my God."

Now the last thing shall call your attention to in this model prayer is this, that *the prophet uses argument.* Praying ought always to be made up of arguing. "Bring forth your strong reasons" is a good canon for a prevalent prayer. We should urge matters with God and bring reasons before Him—not because He wants reasons, but He desires us to know why we desire the blessing. In this text we have a reason given, first—

"Defer not for thine own sake," as much as if he had said, "If You suffer this people of Yours to perish, all the world will revile Your name; Your honor will be stained. This is Your own people, and because they are Your property, suffer not Your own estate to be endangered, but save Jerusalem for Your own sake."

Then next, he puts it on the same footing in another shape, "For thy city and thy people"; he urges that this people were not like other people. They had sinned truly, but still there was a relationship between them and God that existed between God and no other people. He pleads the covenant, in fact, between Abraham and Abraham's seed and the God of the whole earth. Good pleading that! And then he puts in next, "For they are called by thy name." They were said to be Jehovah's people; they were named by the name of the God of Israel. "O God! let not a thing that bears Your name be trundled about like a common thing. Suffer it not to be trailed in the dust; come to the rescue of it. Your stamp, Your seal is upon Israel. Israel belongs to You; therefore, come and interpose." Now from this I gather that if we would prevail, we should plead arguments with God, and these are very many; discreet minds when they are fervent will readily know how far to go in pleading and where to stop. I remember one morning a dear brother, now present, praying in a way that seemed to me to be very prevalent when he spoke thus, "O Lord, You have been pleased to call Your church Your Bride; now we, being evil, have such love toward our spouse that if there were anything in the world that would be for her good, we would not spare to give it to her; will You not, O Husband of the church, do the like with Your spouse, and let Your church receive a blessing now that she pleads for it?" It seemed good arguing, after Christ's own sort, "If ye then, being evil, know how to give good gifts unto your children: how much more shall your heavenly Father give the Holy Spirit to them that ask him?" Get a promise and spread it before the Lord and say, "O Lord, You have said it; do it." God loves to be believed in. He loves you to think He means what He says. He is a practical God Himself. His Word has power in it, and He does not like us to treat His promises as some of us do, as if they were wastepaper, as if they were things to be read for the encouragement of our enthusiasm but not to be used as matters of real practical truth. Oh! plead them with God; fill your mouths with reasonings and come before Him. Make this your determination, that as a church, seeing we need His Spirit and need renewed prosperity, we will not spare nor leave a single argument unused by which we may prevail with the God of mercy to send us what we want. Thus much, then, upon this as a model prayer. Now I shall want a little longer time to speak upon the encouragement that the text and its surroundings give to us in prayer.

Encouragements to Prayer

Brethren, it is always an encouragement to do a thing *when you see the best of men doing it.* Many a person has taken a medicine only because he has known wiser men than himself take it. The best and wisest of persons in all ages have adopted the custom of prayers in times of distress, and, indeed, in all times. That ought to encourage us to do the same. I heard a dear Welsh brother speak last Thursday evening, who interested and amused me too, but I cannot profess to repeat the way in which he told us a biblical story. It was something in this way. He told it as a Welshman, and not quite as I think I might. He said that after the Lord Jesus Christ had gone up to heaven, having told His disciples to wait at Jerusalem until the Spirit of God was given, Peter might have said, "Well, now we must not go out preaching until this blessing comes, so I shall be off fishing." And John might have said, "Well, there is the old boat over at the lake of Gennesaret; I think I shall go and see how that is getting on; it is a long time since I saw after it." And each one might have said, "Well, I shall go about my business, for it is not many days hence when it is coming, and we may as well be at our earthly calling." "No," says he, "they did not say that at all, but Peter said, 'Where shall we hold a prayer meeting?' and Mary said she had got a nice large room that would do for a prayer meeting. True it was in a back street, and the house was not very respectable, and, 'Besides,' says she, 'it is up at the very top of the house, but it is a big room.' 'Never mind,' says Peter, 'it will be nearer to heaven.' So they went into the upper room and there began to pray and did not cease the prayer meeting until the blessing came."

Then the brother told us the next story of a prayer meeting in the Bible. Peter was in prison, and Herod was so afraid that he would get out again that he had sixteen policemen to look after him, and the brethren knew they could not get Peter out in any other way than one; so they said, "We will hold a prayer meeting." Always the way with the church at that time, when anything was amiss, to say, "Where shall we have a prayer meeting?" So Mistress Mark said she had gotten a good room which would do very well for a prayer meeting. It was in a back street, so nobody would know of it, and they would be quiet. So they held that prayer meeting and began to pray. I do not suppose they prayed the Lord to knock the prison walls down nor to kill the policemen nor anything of that kind, but they only prayed that Peter might get out, and they left how he was to get out to God. While they were praying, there came a knock at the door. "Ah!" said they, "that is a policeman come after another of us." But Rhoda went to the door to look, and when she looked she started back in affright. What could she see? She looked again, however, and she was persuaded that it was no other than Peter.

She went back to her mistress and said, "There is Peter at the gate." Good souls! they had been praying that Peter might come out, but they could not believe it, and they said, "Why, it is his spirit—his angel." "No," said the girl, "I know Peter well enough; he has been here dozens of times, and I know it *is* Peter"; and in came Peter, and they all wondered at their unbelief. They had asked God to set Peter free, and free Peter was. It was the prayer meeting that did it. And rest assured we should, everyone, find it our best resource in every hour of need to draw near to God.

> Prayer makes the darkest cloud withdraw,
> Prayer mounts the ladder Jacob saw,
> Gives exercise to faith and love,
> Brings every blessing from above.
>
> Restraining prayer, we cease to fight;
> Prayer makes the Christian armor bright;
> And Satan trembles when he sees
> The weakest saint upon his knees.

It is prayer that does it, and this fact should encourage us to pray.

The success of Daniel's prayer is the next encouragement. He had not gotten to the end of his prayer before a soft hand touched him, and he looked up, and there stood Gabriel in the form of a man. That was quick work surely. So Daniel thought, but it was much quicker than Daniel expected, for as soon as ever he began to pray, the word went forth for the angel to descend. The answer to prayer is the most rapid thing in the world. "Before they call, I will answer; and while they are yet speaking, I will hear." I believe electricity travels at the rate of two hundred thousand miles in a second—so it is estimated; but prayer travels faster than that, for it is, "Before they call, I will answer." There is no time occupied at all. When God wills to answer, the answer may come as soon as the desire is given. And if it delay, it is only that it may come at a better time—like some ships that come home more slowly because they bring the heavier cargo. Delayed prayers are prayers that are put out to interest awhile, to come home, not only with the capital, but with the compound interest too. Oh! prayer cannot fail—prayer cannot fail. Heaven may as soon fall as prayer fail. God may sooner change the ordinances of day and night than He can cease to reply to the faithful, believing, spirit-wrought prayer of His own quickened, earnest, importunate people. Therefore, because He sends success, brethren, pray much.

It ought to encourage us, too, in the next place, to recollect that *Daniel prayed for a very hard case.* Jerusalem was in ruins; the Jews were scattered; their sins were excessive; nevertheless, he prayed, and

God heard him. We are not in so bad a case as that with the church; we have not to mourn that God has departed from us; our prayer is that He may not, even in any measure, withdraw His hand. I do pray God that I may long be buried before He shall suffer this church to lose His presence. There is nothing that I know of in connection with our church life that is worth a single farthing if the Spirit of God be gone. He must be there. Brethren, if you are not prayerful, if you are not holy, if you are not earnest, God does not keep priests, deacons, elders, and church members living near to Him. The sorrow of heart that one will feel if one be kept right himself cannot be expressed. May the Lord prevent our declining. If you are declining, may He bring you back. Some of you, I am afraid, are so getting cold. Now and then I hear of a person who finds it too far to come to the Tabernacle. It used to be very short one time, though it was four or five miles. But when the heart gets cold, the road gets long. Ah! there are some who want this little attention and the other. Time was when they stood in the aisle, in the coldest and draftiest place—if the Word was blessed to them, they would not have minded it. May God grant that you may be a living people always, for years and years to come, until Christ Himself comes. But oh! you that are living near to God, make this your daily, hourly, nightly prayer, that He would not withdraw from us for our sins, but continue to stretch out His hand in loving-kindness, even until He gathers us to our Father.

It ought, further, to encourage us in prayer to remember that *Daniel was only one man, and yet he won his suit.* But if two of you agree as touching any one thing, it shall be done—but a threefold cord—a fifty-fold cord—oh! if, out of our four thousand members, everyone prayed instantly, day and night, for the blessing, oh! what prevalence there must be! Would God it were so!

Brethren, how about your private prayers, are they what they should be? Those morning prayers, those evening prayers, and that midday prayer (for surely your soul must go up to heaven, even if your knees are not bent), are those prayers as they should be? It will bring leanness upon you; there cannot be a fat soul and neglected prayer. There must be much praying if there be much rejoicing in the Lord.

And then your family prayers, do you keep them up? I was in a railway carriage the other day, and a gentleman said to me, who was sitting beside me, "My son is going to be married tomorrow—going to be married to one of your members." "I am glad to hear it," I said. "I hope he is a believer." "Oh! yes, sir; he has been a member of your church for some years. I wish you would write me something to give them tomorrow." Well, you know how the carriage will shake, but I managed to jot down something on a little bit of paper with a pencil. The words, I think, that I put were something like this, "I wish you every joy. May your joys be doubled; may your sorrow be divided and lightened." But then I put, "Build the altar before you build the tent. Take care that daily prayer begins your matrimonial life." I am sure we cannot expect our children to grow up a godly seed if there is no family prayer. Are your family prayers, then, what they ought to be?

Then next, let me say to each one, how about your prayers as members of the church? Perhaps I am the last person that might complain about a prayer meeting. It really is a grand sight to see so many of you, but I must confess I don't feel quite content, for there are some members whom I used to see, but don't see now. I know I see some fresh ones, and we are never short of praying men, but I want to see the others as well. I know those who are constantly at prayer meetings can say it is good to be there. It is the best evening in the week often to us when we come together to entreat for the blessing. Do not, I pray you, get into the habit of neglecting the assembling of yourselves together for prayer. How often have I said, "All our strength lies in prayer"! When we were very few, God multiplied us in answer to prayer. What prayers we put up night and day when we launched out to preach the Gospel in a larger building! And what an answer God sent us. Since then, in times of need and trouble we have cried to God, and He has heard us. Daily He sends us help for our college, for our orphanage, and for our other works, in answer to prayer. Oh! you that come here as members of the church, if you do not pray, the very beams out of these walls and the stones will cry out against you. This house was built in answer to prayer. If anybody had said that we, who were but few and poor, could have erected such a structure, I think it would have sounded impossible. But it was done— you know how readily it was done, how God raised us up friends, how He has helped us to this day. Oh! don't stop your prayers. You seem to me, good people, to be very like that king who, when he went to the dying prophet, was told, Take your arrows and smite upon the ground. And he struck thrice and he stopped, and the prophet was angry and said, You should have struck many times, and then you would have utterly destroyed your enemies. And so we pray, as it were, but little. We ask but little, and God gives it. Oh! that we could ask much and pray for much and strike many times, and plead very earnestly.

Look at this city of ours. I would not say a word in derogation of my country, but I am afraid there is not much to choose between the sin of London and the sin of Paris. And see what has come on Paris! One could hardly live in that city and know all the sin that was going on there without fearing that national sin would bring a national chastisement. And oh! this wicked city of London, with its dens of vice and filthiness! You are the salt of the earth; you that love Christ, let not your salt lose its savor. God forbid that you should sin against the Lord by ceasing to pray for this wicked people. Everywhere, sea and land, is compassed by the ad-versaries of the truth to make proselytes. I beseech you, compass the mercy seat that their machinations may be defeated. At this time there ought to be special prayer. When God in providence seems to be shaking the papacy to its base, now should we cry aloud and spare not. Out of these convulsions God may bring lasting blessings. Let us not neglect to work when God works. Let the hand of the man be lifted up in prayer when the wing of the angel is moved in providence. We may expect great things if we can pray greatly and wrestle earnestly. I call you, in God's name, to the mercy seat. Draw near thither with intense importu-nity, and such a blessing shall come as you have not yet imagined. Pray for some here present that are unconverted. There are a good many of them. They will not pray for themselves; let us pray them into prayer; let us pray God for them, until they at last pray God for themselves. Prayer can mercy's door unlock, for others as well as for our own persons; let us, therefore, abound in prayer, and God send us the blessing, for Jesus' sake. Amen.

9

"Lead Us Not into Temptation"

Lead us not into temptation (Matthew 6:13).

L ooking over a book of addresses to young people the other day, I met with the outline of a discourse that struck me as being a perfect gem. I will give it to you. The text is the Lord's Prayer, and the exposition is divided into most instructive heads. "Our Father which art in heaven": *a child away from home.* "Hallowed be thy name": *a worshiper.* "Thy kingdom come": *a subject.* "Thy will be done in earth, as it is in heaven": *a servant.* "Give us this day our daily bread": *a beggar.* "And forgive us our debts, as we forgive our debtors": *a sinner.* "And lead us not into temptation, but deliver us from evil": *a sinner in danger of being a greater sinner still.* The titles are in every case most appropriate and truthfully condense the petition.

Now if you will remember the outline you will notice that the prayer is like a ladder. The petitions begin at the top and go downward. "Our Father which art in heaven": a child, a child of the heavenly Father. Now to be a child of God is the highest possible position of man. "Behold, what manner of love the Father hath bestowed upon us, that we should be called the sons of God." This is what Christ is—the Son of God, and "our Father" is but a plural form of the very term that He uses in addressing God, for Jesus says, "Father." It is a very high, gracious, exalted position that by faith we dare to occupy when we intelligently say, "Our Father which art in heaven."

It is a step down to the next—"Hallowed be thy name." Here we have a worshiper adoring with lowly reverence the thrice holy God. A worshiper's place is a high one, but it attains not to the excellence of the

---

This sermon was taken from *The Metropolitan Tabernacle Pulpit* and was preached at the Metropolitan Tabernacle, Newington, in 1878.

child's position. Angels come as high as being worshipers; their incessant song hallows the name of God, but they cannot say, "Our Father," "For unto which of the angels said he . . . , Thou art my Son"? They must be content to be within one step of the highest, but they cannot reach the summit, for neither by adoption, regeneration, nor by union to Christ are they the children of God. "Abba, Father," is for men, not for angels, and therefore the worshiping sentence of the prayer is one step lower than the opening, "Our Father."

The next petition is for us as subjects, "Thy kingdom come." The subject comes lower than the worshiper, for worship is an elevated engagement wherein man exercises a priesthood and is seen in lowly but honorable estate. The child worships and then confesses the Great Father's royalty.

Descending still, the next position is that of a servant, "Thy will be done in earth, as it is in heaven." That is another step lower than a subject, for her majesty the queen has many subjects who are not her servants. They are not bound to wait upon her in the palace with personal service though they own her as their honored sovereign. Dukes and such like are her subjects, but not her servants. The servant is a grade below the subject.

Everyone will own that the next petition is lower by far, for it is that of a beggar: "Give us this day our daily bread"—a beggar for bread—an everyday beggar—one who has continually to appeal to charity, even for his livelihood. This is a fit place for us to occupy who owe our all to the charity of heaven.

But there is a step lower than the beggar's, and that is the sinner's place. "Forgive" is lowlier than "give." "Forgive us our debts, as we forgive our debtors." Here too we may each one take up his position, for no word better befits our unworthy lips than the prayer "Forgive." As long as we live and sin we ought to weep and cry, "Have mercy on us, O Lord."

And now, at the very bottom of the ladder, stands a sinner, afraid of yet greater sin, in extreme danger and in conscious weakness, sensible of past sin and fearful of it for the future; hear him as with trembling lip he cries in the words of our text, "Lead us not into temptation, but deliver us from evil."

And yet, dear friends, though I have thus described the prayer as a going downward, downward is in matters of grace much the same as upward, as we could readily show if time permitted. At any rate the downgoing process of the prayer might equally well illustrate the advance of the divine life in the soul. The last clause of the prayer contains in it a deeper inward experience than the earlier part of it. Every believer is a child of God, a worshiper, a subject, a servant, a beggar, and a sinner, but it is not every man who perceives the allurements that beset him or his own tendency to yield to them. It is not every child of God, even when advanced in years, who knows to the full the meaning of being led into temptation, for some follow an easy path and are seldom buffeted; others are such tender babes that they hardly know their own corruptions. Fully to understand our text a man should have had sharp brushes in the wars and have done battle against the enemy within his soul for many a day. He who has escaped as by the skin of his teeth offers this prayer with an emphasis of meaning. The man who has felt the fowler's net about him—the man who has been seized by the adversary and almost destroyed—he prays with awful eagerness, "Lead us not into temptation."

I purpose at this time, in trying to commend this prayer to you, to notice first of all, *the spirit that suggests such a petition*; secondly, *the trials that such a prayer deprecates*; and then, thirdly, *the lessons that it teaches*.

What Suggests Such a Prayer as "Lead us not into temptation"?

To pray, "Lead us not into temptation," first, from the position of the clause, I gather by a slight reasoning process, that it is suggested by *watchfulness*. This petition follows after the sentence, "Forgive us our debts." I will suppose the petition to have been answered, and the man's sin is forgiven. What then? If you will look back upon your own lives, you will soon perceive what generally happens to a pardoned man, for "As in water face answereth to face, so the heart of man to man." One believing man's inner experience is like another's, and your own feelings were the same as mine. Very speedily after the penitent has received forgiveness and has the sense of it in his soul he is tempted of the Devil, for Satan cannot bear to lose his subjects, and when he sees them cross the borderline and escape out of his hand, he gathers up all his forces and exercises all his cunning if, perchance, he may slay them at once. To meet this special assault the Lord makes the heart watchful. Perceiving the ferocity and subtlety of Satan's temptations, the newborn believer, rejoicing in the perfect pardon he has received, cries to God, "Lead us not into temptation." It is the fear of losing the joy of pardoned sin that thus cries out to the good Lord—"Our Father, do not suffer us to lose the salvation we have so lately obtained. Do not even subject it to jeopardy. Do not permit Satan to break our newfound peace. We have but newly escaped, do not plunge us in the deeps again. Swimming to shore, some on boards and some on broken pieces of the ship, we have come safe to land; constrain us not to tempt the boisterous main again. Cast us not upon the rough billows anymore. O God we see the Enemy advancing: he is ready if he can to sift us as wheat. Do not suffer us to be put into his sieve, but deliver us, we pray Thee." It is a prayer of watchfulness; mark you, though we have spoken of watchfulness as necessary at the commencement of the Christian life, it is equally needful even to the close. There is no hour in which a believer can afford to slumber. Watch, I pray you, when you are alone, for temptation, like a creeping assassin, has its dagger for solitary hearts. You must bolt and bar the door well if you would keep out the Devil. Watch yourself in public, for temptations in troops cause their arrows to fly by day. The choicest companions you can select will not be without some evil influence upon you unless you be on your guard. Remember our blessed Master's words, "What I say unto you I say unto all, Watch," and as you watch this prayer will often rise from your inmost heart:

> From dark temptation's power,
>   From Satan's wiles defend;
> Deliver in the evil hour,
>   And guide me to the end.

It is the prayer of watchfulness.

Next, it seems to me to be the natural prayer of *holy horror at the very thought of falling again into sin*. I remember the story of a pitman who, having been a gross blasphemer, a man of licentious life and everything that was bad, when converted by divine grace, was terribly afraid lest his old companions should lead him back again. He knew himself to be a man of strong passions and very apt to be led astray by others, and therefore in his dread of being drawn into his old sins, he prayed most vehemently that sooner than ever he should go back to his old ways he might die. He did die there and then. Perhaps it was the best answer to the best prayer that the poor man could have offered. I am sure any man who has once lived an evil life, if the wondrous grace of God has snatched him from it, will agree that the pitman's prayer was not one whit too enthusiastic. It were better for us to die at once than to live on and return to our first estate and bring dishonor upon the name of Jesus Christ our Lord. The prayer before us springs from the shrinking of the soul at the first approach of the tempter. The footfall of the fiend falls on the startled ear of the timid penitent; he quivers like an aspen leaf and cries out, What, is he coming again? And is it possible that I may fall again? And may I once more defile these garments with that loathsome murderous sin that slew my Lord? "O my God," the prayer seems to say, "keep me from so dire an evil. Lead me, I pray, where You will—aye, even through death's dark valley, but do not lead me into temptation, lest I fall and dishonor You." The burned child dreads the fire. He who has once been caught in the steel trap carries the scars in his flesh and is horribly afraid of being again held by its cruel teeth.

The third feeling, also, is very apparent, namely, *diffidence of personal strength*. The man who feels himself strong enough for anything is daring and even invites the battle that will prove his power. "Oh," says he, "I care not; they may gather about me who will; I am quite able to take care of myself and hold my own against any number." He is ready to be led into conflict; he courts the fray. Not so the man who has been taught of God and has learned his own weakness; he does not want to be tried but seeks quiet places where he may be out of harm's way. Put him into the battle and he will play the man, let him be tempted and you will see how steadfast he will be, but he does not ask for conflict, as, I think, few soldiers will who know what fighting means. Surely it is only those who have never smelled gunpowder or seen the corpses heaped in bloody masses on each other that are so eager for the shot and shell, but your veteran would rather enjoy the piping times of peace. No experienced believer ever desires spiritual conflict, though perchance some raw recruits may challenge it. In the Christian a recollection of his previous weakness—his resolutions broken, his promises unkept—makes him pray that he may not in future be severely tested. He does not dare to trust himself again. He wants no fight with Satan or with the world, but he asks that if possible he may be kept from those severe encounters, and his prayer is, "Lead us not into temptation." The wise believer shows a sacred diffidence—no, I think I may say an utter despair of himself; even though he knows that the power of God is strong enough for anything, yet is the sense of his weakness so heavy upon him that he begs to be spared too much trial. Hence the cry, "Lead us not into temptation."

Nor have I quite exhausted, I think, the phases of the spirit which suggests this prayer, for it seems to me to arise somewhat out of *charity*. "Charity?" say you. "How so?" Well, the connection is always to be observed, and by reading the preceding sentence in connection with it we get the words, "as we forgive our debtors, and lead us not into temptation." We should not be too severe with those persons who have done wrong and have offended us, but pray, "Lord, lead us not into temptation." Your maidservant, poor girl, did purloin a trifle from your property. I make no excuse for her theft, but I beseech you pause awhile before you quite ruin her character for life. Ask yourself, "Might not I have done the same had I been in her position? Lord, lead me not into temptation." It is true it was very wrong in that young man to deal so dishonestly with your goods. Still, you know, he was under great pressure from a strong hand and only yielded from compulsion. Do not be too severe. Do not say, "I will push the matter through; I will have the law of him." No, but wait awhile; let pity speak, let mercy's silver voice plead with you. Remember yourself, lest you also be tempted, and pray "Lead us not into temptation." I am afraid that badly as some behave under temptation, others of us might have done worse if we had been there. I like, if I can, to form a kind judgment of the erring; it helps me to do so when I imagine myself to have been subject to their trials and to have looked at things from their point of view and to have been in their circumstances and to have nothing of the grace of God to help me; should I not have fallen as badly as they have done or even gone beyond them in evil?

May not the day come to you who show no mercy in which you may have to ask mercy for yourselves? Did I say—may it not come to you? No, it must come to you. When leaving all below, you will have to take a retrospective view of your lives and see much to mourn over; to what can you appeal then but to the mercy of God? And what if He should answer you, "An appeal was made to your mercy, and you had none. As you rendered to others, so will I render to you." What answer would you have if God were so to treat you? Would not such an answer be just and right? Should not every man be paid in his own coin when he stands at the judgment seat? So I think that this prayer, "Lead us not into temptation," should often spring up from the heart through a charitable feeling toward others who have erred, who are of the same flesh and blood as ourselves. Now, whenever you see the drunkard reel through the streets, do not glory over him but say, "Lead us not into temptation." When you take down the papers and read that men of position have betrayed their trust for gold, condemn their conduct if you will, but do not exult in your own steadfastness; rather, cry in all humility, "Lead us not into temptation." When the poor girl seduced from the paths of virtue comes across your way, look not on her with the scorn that would give her up to destruction, but say, "Lead us not into temptation." It would teach us milder and gentler ways with sinful men and women if this prayer were as often in our hearts as it is upon our lips.

Once more, do you not think that this prayer breathes the spirit of *confidence*—confidence in God? "Why," says one, "I do not see that." To me—I know not whether I shall be able to convey my thought—to me there is a degree of very tender familiarity and sacred boldness in this expression. Of course, God will lead me now that I am His child. Moreover, now that He has forgiven me, I know that He will not lead me where I can come to any harm. This my faith ought to know and believe, and yet for several reasons there rises to my mind a fear lest His providence should conduct me where I shall be tempted. Is that fear right or wrong? It burdens my mind; may I go with it to my God? May I express in prayer this misgiving of soul? May I pour out this anxiety before the great, wise, loving God? Will it not be impertinent? No, it will not, for Jesus puts the words into my mouth and says, "After this manner therefore pray ye." You are afraid that He may lead you into temptation, but He will not do so; should He see fit to try you, He will also afford you strength to hold out to the end. He will be pleased in His infinite mercy to preserve you. Where He leads it will be perfectly safe for you to follow, for His presence will make the deadliest air to become healthful. But since instinctively you have a dread lest you should be conducted where the fight will be too stern and the way too rough, tell it to your heavenly Father without reserve.

You know at home if a child has any little complaint against his father it is always better for him to tell it. If he thinks that his father overlooked him the other day or half thinks that the task his father has given him is too severe or fancies that his father is expecting too much of him—if he does not say anything at all about it, he may sulk and lose much of the loving tenderness which a child's heart should always feel. But when the child frankly says, "Father, I do not want you to think that I do not love you or that I cannot trust you, but I have a troublous thought in my mind, and I will tell it right straight out"; that is the wisest course to follow and shows a filial trust. That is the way to keep up love and confidence. So if you have a suspicion in your soul that perhaps your Father might put you into temptation too strong for you, tell it to Him. Tell it to Him, though it seems taking a great liberty. Though the fear may be the fruit of unbelief yet make it known to your Lord, and do not harbor it sullenly. Remember the Lord's Prayer was not made for Him but for you, and therefore it reads matters from your standpoint and not from His. Our Lord's Prayer is not for our Lord; it is for us, His children, and children say to their fathers ever so many things that it is quite proper for them to say but that are not wise and accurate after the measure of their parents' knowledge. Their fathers know what their hearts mean, and yet there may be a good deal in what they say that is foolish or mistaken. So I look upon this prayer as exhibiting that blessed childlike confidence that tells out to its father a fear that grieves it, whether that fear be altogether correct or not. Beloved, we need not here debate the question whether God does lead into temptation or not or whether we can fall from grace or not; it is enough that we have a fear and are permitted to tell it to our Father in heaven. Whenever you have a fear of any kind, hurry off with it to Him who loves His little ones and, like a father, pities them and soothes even their needless alarms.

Thus have I shown that the spirit that suggests this prayer is that of watchfulness, of holy horror at the very thought of sin, of diffidence of our own strength, of charity toward others, and of confidence in God.

What Temptations?

What are these temptations that the prayer deprecates? I do not think the prayer is intended at all to ask God to spare us from being afflicted for our good or to save us from being made to suffer as a chastisement. Of course we should be glad to escape those things, but the prayer aims at another form of trial and may be paraphrased thus—"Save me, O Lord, from such trials and sufferings as may lead me into sin. Spare me from too great trials, lest I fall by their overcoming my patience, my faith, or my steadfastness."

Now, as briefly as I can, I will show you how men may be led into temptation by the hand of God.

We may be led into temptation first, *by the withdrawal of divine grace.* Suppose for a moment—it is only a supposition—suppose the Lord were to leave us altogether, then should we perish speedily; but suppose—and this is not a barren supposition—that He were in some measure to take away His strength from us, should we not be in an evil case? Suppose He did not support our faith; what unbelief we should exhibit? Suppose He refused to support us in the time of trial so that we no longer maintained our integrity; what would become of us? Ah, the most upright man would not be upright long, nor the most holy, holy anymore. Suppose, dear friend—you who walk in the light of God's countenance and bear life's yoke so easily because He sustains you— suppose His presence were withdrawn from you, what must be your portion?

We are all so like to Samson in this matter that I must bring him in as the illustration, though he has often been used for that purpose by others. So long as the locks of our heads are unshorn we can do anything and everything—we can rend lions, carry gates of Gaza, and smite the armies of the alien. It is by the divine consecrating mark that we are strong in the power of His might, but if the Lord be once withdrawn and we attempt the work alone, then are we weak as the tiniest insect. When the Lord has departed from you, O Samson, what are you more than another man? Then the cry, "The Philistines be upon thee, Samson," is the knell of all your glory. You vainly shake those lusty limbs of yours. Now you will have your eyes put out, and the Philistines will make sport of you. In view of a like catastrophe we may well be in an agony of supplication. Pray then, "Lord, leave me not; lead me not into temptation by taking Your Spirit from me."

> Keep us, Lord, oh keep us ever,
>   Vain our hope if left by thee
> We are thine, oh leave us never,
>   Till thy face in heaven we see;

> There to praise thee
> > Through a bright eternity.
>
> All our strength at once would fail us,
> > If deserted, Lord, by thee;
> Nothing then could aught avail us,
> > Certain our defeat would be.
> Those who hate us
> > Thenceforth their desire would see.

Another set of temptations will be found in *providential conditions.* The words of Agur, the son of Jakeh, shall be my illustration here. "Remove far from me vanity and lies: give me neither poverty nor riches; feed me with food convenient for me: lest I be full, and deny thee, and say, Who is the Lord? or lest I be poor, and steal, and take the name of my God in vain." Some of us have never known what actual want means but have from our youth up lived in social comfort. Dear friends, when we see what extreme poverty has made some men do, how do we know that we should not have behaved even worse if we had been as sorely pressed as they? We may well shudder and say, "Lord, when I see poor families crowded together in one little room where there is scarcely space to observe common decency, when I see hardly bread enough to keep the children from crying for hunger, when I see the man's garments wearing out upon his back and by far too thin to keep out the cold, I pray You, subject me not to such trial, lest if I were in such a case I might put forth my hand and steal. Lead me not into the temptation of pining want."

And, on the other hand, look at the temptations of money when men have more to spend than they can possibly need, and there is around them a society that tempts them into racing and gambling and whoredom and all manner of iniquities. The young man who has a fortune ready to hand before he reaches years of discretion and is surrounded by flatterers and tempters all eager to plunder him—do you wonder that he is led into vice and becomes a ruined man morally? Like a rich galleon waylaid by pirates, he is never out of danger; is it a marvel that he never reaches the port of safety? Women tempt him, men flatter him, vile messengers of the Devil fawn upon him, and the young simpleton goes after them like an ox to the slaughter or as a bird hastens to the snare and knows not that it is for his life. You may very well thank heaven you never knew the temptation, for if it were put in your way, you would also be in sore peril. If riches and honor allure you, follow not eagerly after them, but pray, "Lead us not into temptation."

Providential positions often try men. There is a man very much pushed for ready money in business; how shall he meet that heavy bill? If he does not meet it, there will be desolation in his family; the mercantile concern from which he now draws his living will be broken up; everybody will be ashamed of him; his children will be outcasts; and he will be ruined. He has only to use a sum of trust money; he has no right to risk a penny of it, for it is not his, but still by its temporary use he may perchance tide over the difficulty. The Devil tells him he can put it back in a week. If he does touch that money, it will be a roguish action, but then he says, "Nobody will be hurt by it, and it will be a wonderful accommodation," and so on. If he yields to the suggestion and the thing goes right, there are some who would say, "Well, after all, there was not much harm in it, and it was a prudent step, for it saved him from ruin." But if it goes wrong, and he is found out, then everybody says, "It was a shameful robbery. The man ought to be transported." But, brethren, the action was wrong in itself, and the consequences neither make it better nor worse. Do not bitterly condemn, but pray again and again, "Lead us not into temptation. Lead us not into temptation." You see God does put men into such positions in providence at times that they are severely tried. It is for their good that they are tried, and when they can stand the trial, they magnify His grace, and they themselves become stronger men; the test has beneficial uses when it can be borne, and God therefore does not always screen His children from it. Our heavenly Father has never meant to cuddle us up and keep us out of temptation, for that is no part of the system that He has wisely arranged for our education. He does not mean us to be babies in go-carts all our lives. He made Adam and Eve in the Garden, and He did not put an iron palisade around the Tree of Knowledge and say, "You cannot get at it." No, He warned them not to touch the fruit, but they could reach the tree if they would. He meant that they should have the possibility of attaining the dignity of voluntary fidelity if they remained steadfast, but they lost it by their sin; God means in His new creation not to shield His people from every kind of test and trial, for that were to breed hypocrites and to keep even the faithful weak and dwarfish. The Lord does sometimes put the chosen where they are tried, and we do right to pray, "Lead us not into temptation."

And there are temptations arising out of *physical conditions*. There are some men who are very moral in character because they are in health; there are other men who are very bad, who, I do not doubt, if we knew all about them, should have some little leniency shown them because of the unhappy conformation of their constitution. Why, there are many people to whom to be cheerful and to be generous is no effort whatsoever, while there are others who need to labor hard to keep themselves from despair and misanthropy. Diseased livers, palpitating hearts, and injured brains are hard things to struggle against. Does that poor old lady complain? She has only had the rheumatism thirty years, and yet she now and then murmurs! How would you be if you felt her pains for thirty minutes? I have heard of a man who complained to everybody. When he came to die, the doctors opened his skull, and they found a close fitting brainbox and that the man suffered from an irritable brain. Did not that account for a great many of his hard speeches? I do not mention these matters to excuse sin, but to make you and me treat such people as gently as we can, and pray, "Lord, do not give me such a brainbox, and do not let me have such rheumatisms or such pains, because upon such a rack I may be much worse than they are. Lead us not into temptation."

So, again, *mental conditions* often furnish great temptations. When a man becomes depressed, he becomes tempted. Those among us who rejoice much often sink about as much as we rise, and when everything looks dark around us, Satan is sure to seize the occasion to suggest despondency. God forbid that we should excuse ourselves, but, dear brother, pray that you be not led into this temptation. Perhaps if you were as much a subject of nervousness and sinking of spirit as the friend you blame for his melancholy, you might be more blameworthy than he, therefore pity rather than condemn.

And, on the other hand, when the spirits are exhilarated and the heart is ready to dance for joy, it is very easy for levity to step in and for words to be spoken amiss. Pray the Lord not to let you rise so high or sink so low as to be led into evil. "Lead us not into temptation" must be our hourly prayer.

Further than this, there are temptations arising out of *personal associations*, which are formed for us in the order of providence. We are bound to shun evil company, but there are cases in which, without fault on their part, persons are made to associate with bad characters. I may instance the pious child whose father is a swearer, and the godly woman lately converted, whose husband remains a swearer and blasphemes the name of Christ. It is the same with workmen who have to labor in workshops where lewd fellows at every half a dozen words let fall an oath and pour forth that filthy language that shocks us every day more and more. I think that in London our working people talk more filthy than ever they did; at least, I hear more of it as I pass along or pause in the street. Well, if persons are obliged to work in such shops or to live in such families, there may come times when under the lash of jest and sneer and sarcasm the heart may be a little dismayed and the tongue may refuse to speak for Christ. Such a silence and cowardice are not to be excused, yet do not censure your brother, but say, "Lord, lead me not into temptation." How know you that you would be more bold? Peter quailed before a talkative maid, and you may be cowed by a woman's tongue. The worst temptation for a young Christian that I know of is to live with a hypocrite—a man so sanctified and demure that the young heart, deceived by appearances, fully trusts him while the wretch is false at heart and rotten in life. And such wretches there are who, with the pretense and affectation of sanctimoniousness, will do deeds at which we might weep tears of blood; young people are frightfully staggered, and many of them become deformed for life in their spiritual characteristics through associating with such beings as these. When you see faults caused by such common but horrible causes, say to yourself, "Lord, lead me not into temptation. I thank You for godly parents and for Christian associations and for godly examples, but what might I have been if I had been subjected to the very reverse? If evil influences had touched me when like a vessel I was upon the wheel, I might have exhibited even grosser failings than those that I now see in others."

Thus I might continue to urge you to pray, dear friends, against various temptations; but let me say, the Lord has for some men very *special tests*, such as may be seen in the case of Abraham. He gives him a son in his old age and then says to him, "Take now thy son, thine only son Isaac, whom thou lovest, . . . and offer him . . . for a burnt offering." You will do right to pray, "Lord, lead me not into such a temptation as that. I am not worthy to be so tried. Oh, do not so test me." I have known some Christians sit down and calculate whether they could have acted as the patriarch did. It is very foolish, dear brother. When you are called upon to do it, you will be enabled to make the same sacrifice by the grace of God, but if you are not called upon to do it, why should the power be given? Shall God's grace be left unused? Your strength shall be equal to your day, but it shall not exceed it. I would have you ask to be spared the sterner tests.

Another instance is to be seen in Job. God gave Job over to Satan with a limit, and you know how Satan tormented him and tried to overwhelm him. If any man were to pray, "Lord, try me like Job," it would be a very unwise prayer. "Oh, but I could be as patient as he," say you. You are the very man who would yield to bitterness and curse your God. The man who could best exhibit the patience of Job will be the first, according to his Lord's bidding, fervently to pray, "Lead us not into temptation." Dear friends, we are to be prepared for trial if God wills it, but we are not to court it; we are rather to pray against it, even as our Lord Jesus, though ready to drink the bitter cup, yet in an agony exclaimed, "If it be possible, let this cup pass from me." Trials sought after are not such as the Lord has promised to bless. No true child asks for the rod.

To put my meaning in a way in which it will be clearly seen, let me tell an old story. I have read in history that two men were condemned to die as martyrs in the burning days of Queen Mary. One of them boasted very loudly to his companion of his confidence that he should play the man at the stake. He did not mind the suffering; he was so grounded in the Gospel that he knew he should never deny it. He said that he longed for the fatal morning even as a bride for the wedding. His companion in prison in the same chamber was a poor trembling soul who could not and would not deny his Master, but he told his companion that he was very much afraid of the fire. He said he had always been very sensitive of suffering, and he was in great dread that when he began to burn, the pain might cause him to deny the truth. He besought his friend to pray for him, and he spent his time very much in weeping over his weakness and crying to God for strength. The other continually rebuked him and chided him for being so unbelieving and weak. When they both came to the stake, he who had been so bold recanted at the sight of the fire and went back ignominiously to an apostate's life, while the poor trembling man whose prayer had been, "Lead me not into temptation," stood firm as a rock, praising and magnifying God as he was burned to a cinder. Weakness is our strength; our strength is weakness. Cry to God that He try you not beyond your strength, and in the shrinking tenderness of your conscious weakness breathe out the prayer, "Lead us not into temptation." Then if He does lead you into the conflict, His Holy Spirit will strengthen you, and you will be brave as a lion before the adversary. Though trembling and shrinking within yourself before the throne of God, you would confront the very Devil and all the hosts of hell without one touch of fear. It may seem strange, but so the case is.

What Lessons Does This Prayer Teach?

Among the lessons this prayer teaches, the first is this: *Never boast your own strength.* Never say, "Oh, I shall never fall into such follies and sins. They may try me, but they will find more than a match in me." Let not him that puts on his harness boast as though he were putting it off. Never indulge one thought of congratulation as to self-strength. You have no power of your own; you are as weak as water. The Devil has only to touch you in the right place, and you will run according to his will. Only let a loose stone or two be moved and you will soon see that the feeble building of your own natural virtue will come down at a run. Never court temptation by boasting your own capacity.

The next thing is *never desire trial.* Does anybody ever do that? Yes. I heard one say the other day that God had so prospered him for years that he was afraid he was not a child of God, for he found that God's children were chastised, and therefore he almost wished to be afflicted. Dear brother, do not wish for that; you will meet with trouble soon enough. If I were a little boy at home, I do not think I should say to my brother, because he had been whipped, "I am afraid I am not my father's child and fear that he does not love me because I am not smarting under the rod. I wish he would whip me just to let me know his love." No. No child would ever be so stupid. We must not for any reason desire to be afflicted or tried, but must pray, "Lead us not into temptation."

The next thought is *never go into temptation*. The man who prays "Lead us not into temptation," and then goes into it is a liar before God. What a hypocrite a man must be who utters this prayer and then goes off to the theater! How false is he who offers this prayer and then stands at the bar and drinks and talks with depraved men and bedizened women! "Lead us not into temptation" is shameful profanity when it comes from the lips of men who resort to places of amusement whose moral tone is bad. "Oh," say you, "you should not tell us of such things." Why not? Some of you do them, and I make bold to rebuke evil wherever it is found and shall do so while this tongue can move. There is a world of cant about. People go to church and say, "Lead us not into temptation," and then they know where temptation is to be found, and they go straight into it. You need not ask the Lord not to lead you there; He has nothing to do with you. The Devil and you between you will go far enough without mocking God with your hypocritical prayers. The man who goes into sin willfully with his eyes open and then bends his knee and says half a dozen times over in his church on a Sunday morning "Lead us not into temptation" is a hypocrite without a mask upon him. Let him take that home to himself and believe that I mean to be personal to him and to such barefaced hypocrites as he.

The last word is, if you pray God not to lead you into temptation, *do not lead others there*. Some seem to be singularly forgetful of the effect of their example for they will do evil things in the presence of their children and those who look up to them. Now I pray you consider that by ill example you destroy others as well as yourself. Do nothing, my dear brother, of that you have need to be ashamed or which you would not wish others to copy. Do the right at all times, and do not let Satan make a cat's-paw of you to destroy the souls of others. Do you pray, "Lead us not into temptation"? Then do not lead your children there. They are invited during the festive season to such and such a family party where there will be everything but what will conduce to their spiritual growth or even to their good morals, do not allow them to go. Put your foot down. Be steadfast about it. Having once prayed, "Lead us not into temptation," act not the hypocrite by allowing your children to go into it.

God bless these words to us. May they sink into our souls, and if any feel that you have sinned, oh, that you may now ask forgiveness through the precious blood of Christ and find it by faith in Him. When you have obtained mercy, let your next desire be that you may be kept in future from sinning as you did before, and therefore pray, "Lead us not into temptation." God bless you.

10

Peter's Shortest Prayer

Lord, save me (Matthew 14:30).

I am going to talk about the characteristics of this prayer in the hope that there may be many who have never yet prayed aright who may make this their own prayer tonight, so that from many a person here present this cry may silently go up, "Lord, save me."

Where did Peter pray this prayer? It was not in a place set apart for public worship nor in his usual place for private prayer; he prayed this prayer just as he was sinking in the water. He was in great peril, so he cried out, "Lord, save me." It is well to assemble with God's people for prayer if you can, but if you cannot go up to His house, it matters little, for prayer can ascend to Him from anywhere all over the world. It is well to have a special spot where you pray at home; probably most of us have a certain chair by which we kneel to pray, and we feel that we can talk to God most freely there. At the same time, we must never allow ourselves to become the slaves even of such a good habit as that and must always remember that, if we really want to find the Lord by prayer—

> Where'er we seek him, he is found,
> And every place is hallowed ground.

We may pray to God when engaged in any occupation if it is a lawful one; if it is not, we have no business to be in it. If there is anything we do over which we cannot pray, we ought never to dare to do it again; if there is any occupation concerning which we have to say, "We could not pray while engaged in it," it is clear that the occupation is a wrong one.

The habit of daily prayer must be maintained. It is well to have regular hours for devotion and to resort to the same place for prayer as far as possible; still, the spirit of prayer is better even than the habit of prayer.

This sermon was taken from *The Metropolitan Tabernacle Pulpit* and was preached on Thursday evening, October 2, 1873.

It is better to be able to pray at all times than to make it a rule to pray at certain times and seasons. A Christian is more fully grown in grace when he prays about everything than he would be if he only prayed under certain conditions and circumstances. I always feel that there is something wrong if I go without prayer for even half an hour in the day. I cannot understand how a Christian man can go from morning to evening without prayer. I cannot comprehend how he lives and how he fights the battle of life without asking the guardian care of God while the arrows of temptation are flying so thickly around him. I cannot imagine how he can decide what to do in times of perplexity, how he can see his own imperfections or the faults of others, without feeling constrained to say, all day long, "O Lord, guide me; O Lord, forgive me; O Lord, bless my friend!" I cannot think how he can be continually receiving mercies from the Lord without saying, "God be thanked for this new token of His grace! Blessed be the name of the Lord for what He is doing for me in His abounding mercy! O Lord, still remember me with the favor that You show to Your people!" Do not be content, dear brethren and sisters in Christ, unless you can pray everywhere and at all times and so obey the apostolic injunction, "Pray without ceasing."

I have already reminded you, dear friends, that Peter prayed this prayer when he was in circumstances of imminent danger. "Beginning to sink, he cried, saying, Lord, save me." But, asks someone, ought he not to have prayed before? Of course he ought, but if he had not done so, it was not too late. Do not say, concerning any trouble, "Now I am so deeply in it, I cannot go to God about it." Why not? "Is anything too hard for the Lord?" It would have been well if the disciples had prayed before the first rough breath of the tempest began to toss their little bark, yet it was not too late to pray when the vessel seemed as if it must go down. As long as you have a heart to pray, God has an ear to hear. Look at Peter; he is "beginning to sink." The water is up to his knees, it is up to his waist, it is up to his neck, but it is not yet too late for him to cry, "Lord, save me"; he has no sooner said it than the hand of Jesus is stretched out to catch him and to guide him to the ship. So, Christian, cry to God though the Devil tells you it is no use to cry; cry to God even if you are beneath the Tempter's foot. Say to Satan, "Rejoice not against me, O mine enemy: when I fall, I shall arise"; but do not forget to cry to the Lord. Cry to God for your children even when they are most ungodly, when their ungodliness almost breaks your heart. Cry to God on behalf of those whom you are teaching in the Sunday school; even when you seem to think that their characters are developing in the worst possible form, still pray for them. Never mind though the thing you ask for them should appear to be an impossibility, for God "is able to do exceeding abundantly above all that we ask or think."

I would also say to any unconverted person who is here under conviction of sin—dear friend, if you are beginning to sink, yet still pray. If your sins stare you in the face and threaten to drive you to despair, yet still draw near to God in prayer. Though it seems as if hell had opened its mouth to swallow you up, yet still cry to God. While there's life, there's hope.

> While the lamp holds out to burn,
> The vilest sinner may return;

and the vilest sinner who returns shall find that God is both able and willing to save him. Never believe that lie of Satan that prayer will not prevail with God. Only go as the publican did, smiting upon your breast and crying, "God be merciful to me a sinner," and rest assured that God is waiting to be gracious to you.

I cannot help feeling that Peter's short, simple prayer was uttered in a most natural tone of voice, "Lord, save me." Let us always pray in just such a way as the Spirit of God dictates to us and as the deep sorrow and humiliation of our hearts naturally suggest to us. Many men who pray in public get into the habit of using certain tones in prayer that are anything but natural, and I am afraid that some even in private fail to pray naturally. Any language that is not natural is bad; the best tone is that which a man uses when he is speaking earnestly and means what he says, and that is the right way to pray. Speak as if you meant it; do not whine it or cant it or intone it, but pour it out of your soul in the most simple, natural fashion that you can. Peter was in too great peril to put any fine language into his prayer; he was too conscious of his danger to consider how he might put his words together, but he just expressed the strong desire of his soul in the simplest manner possible, "Lord, save me"; that prayer was heard, and Peter was saved from drowning, just as a sinner will be saved from hell if he can pray after the selfsame fashion.

Now, coming to Peter's prayer itself, I suggest that it is a suitable prayer for all who are able to pray at all.

Peter's Prayer Was Brief

Peter's prayer was a very brief prayer. There were only three words in it, "Lord, save me." I believe that the excellence of prayer often consists in its brevity. You must have noticed the extreme brevity of most of the prayers that are preserved in Scripture. One of the longest is the prayer of our Savior recorded by John, which would, I suppose, have occupied about five minutes; and there is the prayer of Solomon at the dedication of the temple, which may have taken six minutes. Almost all the other prayers in the Bible are very short ones, and probably, in our public services, we pray far longer than all of them put together. This may, perhaps, be excused when there are many petitions to be presented by one person on behalf of a large congregation, but at our prayer meetings where there are many to speak, I am certain that the longer the prayer is, the worse it is. Of course, there are exceptions to this rule. The Spirit of God sometimes inspires a man in such a way that, if he would keep on praying all night, we should be glad to join with him in that holy exercise, but, as a general rule, the Spirit of God does no such thing. There are some who pray longest when they have least to say and only go on repeating certain pious phrases that become almost meaningless by monotonous reiteration. Remember, dear friends, when you are praying, whether in public or in private, that you have not to teach the Lord a system of theology; He knows far more about that than you do. You have no need to explain to the Lord all the experience that a Christian ought to have, for He knows far better than you do. And there is no necessity for you always to go around all the various agencies and institutions and mission stations. Tell the Lord what is in your heart in as few words as possible and so leave time and opportunity for others to do the same.

I wonder if anyone here ever says, "I have no time for prayer." Dear friend, dare you leave your house in the morning without bowing the knee before God? Can you venture to close your eyes at night and wear the image of death without first commending yourself to the keeping of God during the hours of unconsciousness in sleep? I do not understand how you can live such a careless life as that. But, surely, you did not really mean that you had not to offer such a prayer as Peter's "Lord, save me." How much time does that take, or this? "God be merciful to me a sinner." If you realized your true condition in God's sight, you would find time for prayer somehow or other, for you would feel that you must pray. It never occurred to Peter, as he was beginning to sink, that he had no time for prayer. He felt that he must pray; his sense of danger forced him to cry to Christ, "Lord, save me." And if you feel as you should feel, your sense of need will drive you to prayer, and never again will you say, "I have no time for prayer." It is not a matter of time so much as a matter of heart; if you have the heart to pray, you will find the time.

I would urge you to cultivate the habit of praying briefly all the day. I have told you before of the Puritan who, in a debate, was observed to be making notes; when they were afterward examined, it was found that there was nothing on the paper except these words, "More light, Lord! More light, Lord! More light, Lord!" He wanted light upon the subject under discussion, and therefore he asked the Lord for it, and that is the way to pray. During the day, you can pray, "Give me more grace, God. Subdue my temper, Lord. Lord, save me." Pray thus, and you will be imitating the good example of brevity in prayer which our text sets before you.

Peter's Prayer Was Comprehensive

Peter's prayer was wonderfully comprehensive and adapted for use on many different occasions. It covered all the needs of Peter at that time, and he might have continued to use it as long as he lived. When his Master told him that Satan desired to have him that he might sift him as wheat, he might well have prayed, "Lord, save me." When he had denied his Master and had gone out and wept bitterly, it would have been well for him to pray, "Lord, save me." When he was afterward journeying to and fro, preaching the Gospel, he could still pray, "Lord, save me"; when, at last, he was led out to be crucified for Christ's sake, he could hardly find a better prayer than this with which to close his life, "Lord, save me."

Now, as Peter found this prayer so suitable for him, I commend it to each one of you. Have you been growing rich lately? Then, you will be tempted to become proud and worldly; so pray, "Lord, save me from the evils that so often go with riches; You are giving me this wealth, help me to be a good steward of it and not to make an idol of it." Or are you getting poor? Is your business proving a failure? Are your little savings almost gone? Well, there are perils connected with poverty; so pray, "Lord, save me from becoming envious or discontented; let me be willing to be poor rather than do anything wrong in order to get money." Do you, dear friend, feel that you are not living as near to God as you once did? Is the chilling influence of the world telling upon you? Then pray, "Lord, save me." Have you fallen into some sin that you fear may bring disgrace upon your profession? Well then, before that sin grows greater, cry, "Lord, save me." Have you come to a place where your feet have well-nigh slipped? The precipice is just before you, and you feel that, if some mightier power than your own does not interpose, you will fall to your serious hurt, if not to your destruction. Then, at once breathe the prayer, "Lord, save me." I can commend this prayer to you when you are upon the stormy sea, but it will be equally suitable to you upon the dry land, "Lord, save me." I can commend it as suitable to you when you are near the gates of death, but it is just as much adapted to you when you are in vigorous health, "Lord, save me." And if you can add to the prayer, "and, Lord, save my children and my kinsfolk and my neighbors," it will be even better. Still, for yourself personally, it is an admirable prayer to carry about with you wherever you go, "Lord, save me."

Peter's Prayer Was Direct

Peter's prayer was very direct. It would not have done for Peter just then to have used the many titles which rightly belong to Christ or to have begun asking for a thousand things, but he went straight to the point of his immediate need and cried, "Lord, save me." When one of our dear friends, who has lately gone to heaven, was very ill, one of his sons prayed with him. He began in a very proper way, "Almighty Father, Maker of heaven and earth, our Creator"—but the sick man stopped him and said, "My dear boy, I am a poor sinner, and I want God's mercy; say, 'Lord, save him.'" He wanted his son to get to the point, and I can sympathize with him, for often, when some of our dear brethren have been praying here and have been beating about the bush, I have wished that they would come to the point and ask for what they really needed. They have kept on walking around the house instead of knocking at the door and seeking to enter. Peter's prayer shows us how to go direct to the very heart of the matter, "Lord, save me."

Many persons fail to receive answers to their prayers because they will not go straight to God and confess the sins that they have committed. There was a member of a Christian church who had, on one occasion, fallen very shamefully through drink. He was very penitent, and he asked his pastor to pray for him, but he would not say what his sin had been. The pastor prayed and then told the brother himself to pray. The poor man said, "Lord, You know that I have erred and done wrong," and so on, making a sort of general confession, but that brought him no peace of mind. He felt that he could not go away like that, so he knelt down again and said, "Lord, You know that I was drunk; it was a shameful sin that I committed, but I am truly grieved for it; O Lord, forgive me, for Jesus' sake!" Before his prayer was finished, he had found peace because he had plainly confessed his sin to God and had not sought to hide it any longer. You remember that David could get no peace until he came to the point and prayed, "Deliver me from bloodguiltiness, O God, thou God of my salvation." Before that, he had tried to smother his great sin; but there was no rest for his conscience until he had made a full confession of his guilt, and after that he could say, "The sacrifices of God are a broken spirit: a broken and a contrite heart, O God, thou wilt not despise." Let our prayers, whether for ourselves or others, and especially our confessions of sin, go straight to the point and not go beating about the bush. If any of you have been using forms of prayer that have not obtained for you any answers to your supplications, put them all on one side and just go and tell the Lord plainly what you want. Your prayer will then probably be something like this, "O God, I am a lost sinner! I have been careless about divine things; I have listened to the Gospel, but I have not obeyed it. Lord, forgive me, save me, make me Your child, and let me, and my household too, be Yours forever." That is the way to pray so that God will hear and answer you.

Peter's Prayer Was Sound

Peter's prayer was a very sound-doctrine prayer. Peter does not appear to have had any idea of saving himself from drowning; he does not seem to have thought that there was sufficient natural buoyancy about him to keep him afloat or that he could swim to the ship; but, "beginning to sink, he cried, Lord, save me." One of the hardest tasks in the world is to get a man to give up all confidence in himself and from his heart to pray, "Lord, save me." Instead of doing that, he says, "O Lord, I do not feel as I ought; I want to feel my need more, I want to feel more joy, I want to feel more holiness." You see, he is putting feelings in place of faith; he is, as it were, laying down a track along which he wants God to walk instead of walking in the way that God has marked out for all who desire to be saved. Another man is seeking to reform himself and so to make himself fit for heaven; he prays in harmony with that idea and of course gets no answer. I like to hear such a prayer as this, "O Lord, I cannot save myself, and I do not ask You to save me in any way that I prescribe; Lord, save me anyhow, only do save me! I am satisfied to be saved by the precious blood of Jesus. I am satisfied to be saved by the regenerating work of the Holy Spirit. I know I must be born again if I am ever to enter heaven; quicken me, O ever-blessed Spirit! I know I must give up my sins. Lord, I do not want to keep them, save me from the them by Your grace, I humbly entreat You. I know that only You can do this work; I cannot lift even a finger to help You in it; so save me, Lord, for Your great mercy's sake!" This is sound doctrinal truth—salvation all of grace, not of man, nor by man; "not of blood, nor of the will of the flesh, nor of the will of man, but of God"; salvation according to the eternal purpose of God by the effectual working of the Holy Spirit through the substitutionary sacrifice of Jesus Christ. When a sinner is willing to accept salvation on God's terms, then the prayer shall ascend acceptably to the Most High, "Lord, save me."

Peter's Prayer Was Personal

Peter's prayer was a very personal one. Peter did not think of anybody else just then; and when a soul is under concern about its eternal interests, it had better at first confine its thoughts to itself and pray, "Lord, save *me*." Yes, and in the Christian's afterlife, there will come times when he had better, for a while, forget all others and simply pray, "Lord, save *me*." Here we are, a great congregation, gathered together from very various motives; and perhaps some here, who are not yet personally interested in Christ, are vaguely hoping that God will bless somebody in this assembly; but if the Holy Spirit shall begin to work upon some individual heart and conscience, the convicted one will begin to pray, "Lord, save *me*. I hear of many others being brought to Jesus;

but, Lord, save *me*. My dear sister has been converted and has made a profession of her faith; but, Lord, save *me*. I had a godly mother who has gone home to glory; and my dear father is walking in Your fear; let not their son be a castaway, Lord save *me*."

I entreat everyone here to pray this personal prayer, and I beg you who do love the Lord to join me in pleading with him that it may be so. I see some little girls over there; will not each one of you, my dear children, pray this prayer? I pray the Holy Spirit to move you to cry, "Lord, save little Annie," or "Lord, save little Mary"; and may you boys be equally moved to pray, "Lord, save Tom," or "Lord, save Harry." Pray for yourself in just that simple way, and who knows what blessing may come to you? Then you mothers will surely not let your children pray for themselves, while you remain prayerless; will not each one of you cry, "Lord, save me"? And you working men, whom I am so glad to see at a week night service, do not go away without presenting your own personal petitions. The apostle Peter had to pray for himself; the most eminent servants of God had to pray for themselves, and you must pray for yourselves. If all the saints of God were to pray for you with one united voice as long as you live, you would not be saved unless you also cried to God for yourself. Religion is a personal matter; there is no such thing as religion by proxy. You must repent for yourselves and pray for yourselves and believe for yourselves if you would be saved. May God grant that you may do so!

Peter's Prayer Was Urgent

Peter's prayer was a very urgent one. He did not say, "Lord, save me tomorrow," or "Lord, save me in an hour's time." He was "beginning to sink"; the hungry waves had opened their mouths to swallow him, and he would soon be gone. He had only time to cry, "Lord, save me"; but he no doubt meant, "Lord, save me now, for I am now in danger of being drowned. Lord, save me now; for, if you should delay, I shall sink to the bottom of the sea." "And immediately Jesus stretched forth his hand, and caught him," and so saved him. There are many people who would like Jesus to save them, but when? Ah! that is the point that they have not settled yet. A young man says, "I should like Christ to save me when I grow older, when I have seen a little more of life." You mean when you have seen a great deal more of death, for that is all you will see in the world; there is no real life there except that which is in Christ Jesus. Many a man in middle life has said, "I mean to be a Christian before I die, but not just yet." He has been too busy to seek the Lord, but death has come to him without any warning; busy or not, he has had to die quite unprepared.

There is hope for a sinner when he prays, "Lord, my case is urgent, save me now. Sin, like a viper, has fastened itself upon me; Lord, save me now from its deadly venom. I am guilty now and condemned already, because I have not believed in Jesus; Lord, save me now, save me from condemnation, save me from the damning sin of unbelief. Lord, for aught I know, I am now upon the brink of death, and I am in danger of hell as well as of death as long as I am unforgiven. Therefore, be pleased to let the wheels of your chariot of mercy hasten, and save me even now, O Lord!" I have known some who have been so deeply under the influence of the Holy Spirit that they have knelt down by their bedsides and said, "We will never give sleep to our eyes or slumber to our eyelids until we have found the Savior," and before long they have found Him. They have said, "We will wrestle in prayer until our burden of sin is gone"; and when they have reached that determination, it has not been long before they have obtained the blessing they desired. When nothing else succeeds, importunity will surely prevail. When you will not take a denial from God, He will not give you a denial, but as long as you are content to be unsaved, you will be unsaved. When you cry, with all the urgency of which you are capable, "I must have Jesus or die; I am hungering, thirsting, pining, panting after Him, as the hart pants after the waterbrooks," it shall not be long before you clasp that priceless treasure to your heart and say, "Jesus is my Savior; I have believed in Him."

Peter's Prayer Was Effectual

Peter's prayer was an effectual one. There may be comfort to some here present in the thought that, although this was the prayer of a man in trouble, of a man in whom there was a mixture of unbelief and faith, yet it succeeded. Imperfections and infirmities shall not prevent prayer from speeding if it be but sincere and earnest. Jesus said to Peter, "O thou of little faith, wherefore didst thou doubt?" which shows that he did doubt although there was also some faith in him, for he believed that Christ could save him from a watery grave. Many of us also are strange mixtures, even as Peter was. Repentance and hardness of heart can each occupy a part of our beings, and faith may be in our hearts together with a measure of unbelief, even as it was with the man who said to Jesus, "Lord, I believe; help thou mine unbelief."

Do any of you feel that you want to pray and yet cannot pray? You would believe in Jesus, but there is another law in your members that keeps you back. You would pray an effectual prayer, like that of Elijah, never staggering at the promise through unbelief, but, somehow or other, you cannot tell why, you cannot attain to that prayer. Yet you will not give up praying; you feel that you cannot do that. You linger still at the mercy seat even when you cannot prevail with God in prayer. Ah, dear soul! it is a mercy that God does not judge your prayer by what it is in itself; He judges it from another point of view altogether. Jesus takes it, mends it, adds to it the merit of His own precious blood, and then, when He presents it to His Father, it is so changed that you would scarcely recognize it as your petition. You would say, "I can hardly believe that is my prayer, Christ has so greatly altered and improved it." It has happened to you as it sometimes happens to poor people who are in trouble, as it did happen to one whom I knew some time ago. A good woman wanted me to send in a petition to a certain government office, concerning her husband, who was dead and for whose sake she wanted to get some help. She drew up the petition and brought it to me. About one word in ten was spelled correctly, and the whole composition was unfit to send. She wanted me to add my name to it and post it for her. I did so, but I first rewrote the whole petition, keeping the subject matter as she put it, but altering the form and wording of it. That is what our good Lord and Master does for us, only in an infinitely higher sense; He rewrites our petition, sets His own sign-manual (King's signature) for it, and when His Father sees that, He grants the request at once. One drop of Christ's blood upon a prayer must make it prosper.

Go home therefore, you who are troubled with doubts and fears, you who are vexed by Satan, you who are saddened by the recollection of your own past sins; notwithstanding all this, go to God and say, "Father, I have sinned against heaven, and before thee," and ask for His forgiveness, and His forgiveness you shall receive. Keep on praying in such a fashion as this, "Lord, save me, for Jesus' sake. Jesus, You are the Savior of sinners, save me, I beseech You. You are mighty to save; Lord, save me. You are in heaven pleading for transgressors; Lord, plead for me." Do not wait until you get home, but pray just where you are sitting, "Lord, save me." May God give grace to everyone to pray that prayer from the heart, for Jesus Christ's sake! Amen.

11

The Preparatory Prayers of Christ

Now when all the people were baptized, it came to pass, that Jesus also being baptized, and praying, the heaven was opened, and the Holy Ghost descended in a bodily shape like a dove upon him, and a voice came from heaven, which said, Thou art my beloved Son; in thee I am well pleased (Luke 3:21–22).

And it came to pass in those days, that he went out into a mountain to pray, and continued all night in prayer to God. And when it was day, he called unto him his disciples: and of them he chose twelve, whom also he named apostles (Luke 6:12–13).

And it came to pass about an eight days after these sayings, he took Peter and John and James, and went up into a mountain to pray. And as he prayed, the fashion of his countenance was altered, and his raiment was white and glistering (Luke 9:28–29).

And when he had sent the multitudes away, he went up into a mountain apart to pray: and when the evening was come, he was there alone. But the ship was now in the midst of the sea, tossed with waves: for the wind was contrary. And in the fourth watch of the night Jesus went unto them, walking on the sea (Matthew 14:23–25).

Then they took away the stone from the place where the dead was laid. And Jesus lifted up his eyes, and said, Father, I thank thee that thou hast heard me. And I knew that thou hearest me always: but because of the people which stand by I said it, that they may believe that thou hast sent me (John 11:41–42).

This sermon was taken from *The Metropolitan Tabernacle Pulpit* and was preached on Thursday evening, August 7, 1873.

And the Lord said, Simon, Simon, behold, Satan hath desired to have you, that he may sift you as wheat: but I have prayed for thee, that thy faith fail not: and when thou art converted, strengthen thy brethren (Luke 22:31–32).

And when Jesus had cried with a loud voice, he said, Father, into thy hands I commend my spirit: and having said thus, he gave up the ghost (Luke 23:46).

There is one peculiarity about the life of our Lord Jesus Christ that everybody must have noticed who has carefully read the four Gospels, namely, that He was a man of much prayer. He was mighty as a preacher, for even the officers who were sent to arrest Him said, "Never man spake like this man." But he appears to have been even mightier in prayer, if such a thing could be possible. We do not read that His disciples ever asked Him to teach them to preach, but we are told that, "as he was praying in a certain place, when he ceased, one of His disciples said to Him, Lord, teach us to pray." He had no doubt been praying with such wonderful fervor that His disciples realized that He was a master of the holy art of prayer, and they therefore desired to learn the secret for themselves. The whole life of our Lord Jesus Christ was one of prayer. Though we are often told about His praying, we feel that we scarcely need to be informed of it, for we know that He must have been a man of prayer. His acts are the acts of a prayerful man; His words speak to us like the words of one whose heart was constantly lifted up in prayer to His Father. You could not imagine that He would have breathed out such blessings upon men if He had not first breathed in the atmosphere of heaven. He must have been much in prayer, or He could not have been so abundant in service and so gracious in sympathy.

Prayer seems to be like a silver thread running through the whole of our Savior's life, yet we have the record of His prayers on many special occasions, and it struck me that it would be both interesting and instructive for us to notice some of the seasons that Jesus spent in prayer. I have selected a few that occurred either before some great work or some great suffering, so our subject will really be the preparatory prayers of Christ, the prayers of Christ as He was approaching something that would put a peculiar stress and strain upon His manhood, either for service or for suffering; if the consideration of this subject shall lead all of us to learn the practical lesson of praying at all times and yet to have special seasons for prayer just before any peculiar trial or unusual service, we shall not have met in vain.

Prayer in Preparation for Baptism

Our Lord's prayer in preparation for His baptism is in Luke 3:21–22: "Now when all the people were baptized, it came to pass, that Jesus also being baptized, and praying" (it seems to have been a continuous act in which He had been previously occupied), "the heaven was opened, and the Holy Ghost descended in a bodily shape like a dove upon him, and a voice came from heaven, which said, Thou art my beloved Son; in thee I am well pleased."

The baptism of our Lord was the commencement of His manifestation to the sons of men. He was now about to take upon Himself in full all the works of His messiahship; consequently, we find Him very socially engaged in prayer, and, beloved, it seems to me to be peculiarly appropriate that, when any of us have been converted and are about to make a scriptural profession of our faith—about to take up the soldier life under the great Captain of our salvation—about to start out as pilgrims, to Zion's City bound—I say that it seems to me to be peculiarly appropriate for us to spend much time in very special prayer. I should be very sorry to think that anyone would venture to come to be baptized or to be united with a Christian church without having made that action a matter of much solemn consideration and earnest prayer, but when the decisive step is about to be taken, our whole beings should be very specially concentrated upon our supplications at the throne of grace. Of course, we do not believe in any sacramental efficacy attaching to the observance of the ordinance, but we receive a special blessing in the act itself because we are moved to pray even more than usual before it takes place and at the time. At all events, I know that it was so in my own case. It was many years ago, but the remembrance of it is very vivid at this moment, and it seems to me as though it only happened yesterday. It was in the month of May, and I rose very early in the morning so that I might have a long time in private prayer. Then I had to walk about eight miles from Newmarket to Isleham, where I was to be baptized in the river; I think that the blessing I received that day resulted largely from that season of solitary supplication and my meditation, as I walked along the country roads and lanes, upon my indebtedness to my Savior and my desire to live to His praise and glory. Dear young people, take care that you start right in your Christian life by being much in prayer. A profession of faith that does not begin with prayer will end in disgrace. If you come to join the church, but do not pray to God to uphold you in consistency of life and to make your profession sincere, the probability is that you are already a hypocrite; if that is too uncharitable a suggestion, the probability is that, if you are converted, the work has been of a very superficial character and not of that deep and earnest kind of which prayer would be the certain index. So again I say to you that if any of you are thinking of making a profession of your faith in Christ, be sure that, in preparation for it, you devote a special season to drawing near to God in prayer.

As I read the first text, no doubt you noticed that it was while Christ was praying that "the heaven was opened, and the Holy Ghost descended in a bodily shape like a dove upon him, and a voice came from heaven, which said, Thou art my beloved Son; in thee I am well pleased." There are three occasions of which we read in Scripture when God bore audible testimony to Christ, and on each of these three occasions He was either in the act of prayer or He had been praying but a very short time before. Christ's prayer is specially mentioned in each instance side by side with the witness of His Father, and if you, beloved friends, want to have the witness of God either at your baptism or on any subsequent act of your life, you must obtain it by prayer. The Holy Spirit never sets His seal to a prayerless religion. It has not in it that of which He can approve. It must be truly said of a man, "Behold, he prayeth," before the Lord bears such testimony concerning him as He bore concerning Saul of Tarsus, "He is a chosen vessel unto me, to bear my name before the Gentiles."

So we find that it was while Christ was praying at His baptism that the Holy Spirit came upon Him, "in a bodily shape like a dove," to qualify Him for His public service; it is through prayer that we also receive that spiritual enrichment that equips us as coworkers together with God. Without prayer you will remain in a region that is desolate as a desert, but bend your knees in supplication to the Most High, and you have reached the land of promise, the country of benediction. "Draw nigh to God, and he will draw nigh to you," not merely as to His gracious presence, but as to the powerful and efficacious working of the Holy Spirit. More prayer, more power; the more pleading with God that there is, the more power will there be in pleading with men, for the Holy Spirit will come upon us while we are pleading, and so we shall be fitted and qualified to do the work to which we are called of God.

Let us learn, then, from this first instance of our Savior's preparatory prayer at His baptism the necessity of special supplication on our part in similar circumstances. If we are making our first public profession of faith in Him or if we are renewing that profession, if we are removing to another sphere of service, if we are taking office in the church as deacons or elders, if we are commencing the work of the pastorate, if we are in any way coming out more distinctly before the world as the servants of Christ, let us set apart special seasons for prayer and so seek a double portion of the Holy Spirit's blessing to rest upon us.

Prayer in Preparation for Choosing the Twelve

Our Lord's prayer preparatory to choosing His twelve apostles is recorded in Luke 6:12–13: "And it came to pass in those days, that he went out into a mountain to pray, and continued all night in prayer to God. And when it was day, he called unto him his disciples: and of them he chose twelve, whom also he named apostles."

Our Lord was about to extend His ministry; His one tongue, His one voice, might have delivered His personal message throughout Palestine, but He was desirous of having far more done than He could individually accomplish in the brief period of His public ministry upon the earth. He would therefore have twelve apostles, and afterward seventy disciples, who would go forth in His name and tell out the glad tidings of salvation. He was infinitely wiser than the wisest of mere men, so why did He not at once select His twelve apostles? The men had been with Him from the beginning, and He knew their characters and their fitness for the work He was about to entrust to them; so He might have said to Himself, "I will have James and John and Peter and the rest of the Twelve and send them forth to preach that the kingdom of heaven is at hand and to exercise the miraculous powers with which I will endow them." He might have done this if He had not been the Christ of God, but being the anointed of the Father, He would not take such an important step as that without long-continued prayer. So He went alone to His Father, told Him all that He desired to do, and pleaded with Him, not in the brief fashion that we call prayer, which usually lasts only a few minutes, but His pleading lasted through an entire night.

What our Lord asked for or how He prayed, we cannot tell, for it is not revealed to us, but I think we shall not be guilty of vain or unwarranted curiosity if we use our imaginations for a minute or two. In doing so, with the utmost reverence, I think I hear Christ crying to His Father that the right men might be selected as the leaders of the church of God upon the earth. I think I also hear Him pleading that upon these chosen men a divine influence might rest, that they might be kept in character, honest in heart, and holy in life, and that they might also be preserved sound in doctrine and not turn aside to error and falsehood. Then I think I hear Him praying that success might attend their preaching, that they might be guided where to go, where the blessing of God would go with them, that they might find many hearts willing to receive their testimony, and that, when their personal ministry should end, they might pass on their commission to others, so that, as long as there should be a harvest to be reaped for the Lord, there should be laborers to reap it; as long as there should be lost sinners in the world, there should also be earnest, consecrated men and women seeking to pluck the brands from the burning. I will not attempt to describe the mighty wrestlings of that night of prayer when, in strong crying and tears, Christ poured out His very soul into His Father's ear and heart. But it is clear that He would not dispatch a solitary messenger with the glad tidings of the Gospel unless He was assured that His Father's authority and the Spirit's power would accompany the servants whom He was about to send forth.

What a lesson there is in all this to us! What infallible guidance there is here as to how a missionary society should be conducted! Where there is one committee meeting for business, there ought to be fifty for prayer; whenever we get a missionary society whose main business it is to pray, we shall have a society whose distinguishing characteristic will be that it is the means of saving a multitude of souls. And to you, my dear young brethren in the college, I feel moved to say that I believe we shall have a far larger blessing than we have already had when the spirit of prayer in the college is greater than it now is, though I rejoice to know that it is very deep and fervent even now. You, brethren, have never been lacking in prayerfulness; I thank God that I have never had occasion to complain or to grieve on that account; still, who knows what blessing might follow a night of prayer at the beginning or at any part of the session, or an all-night wrestling in prayer in the privacy of your own bedrooms? Then, when you go out to preach the Gospel on the Sabbath day, you will find that the best preparation for preaching is much praying. I have always found that the meaning of a text can be better learned by prayer than in any other way. Of course, we must consult lexicons and commentaries to see the literal meaning of the words and their relation to one another, but when we have done all that, we shall still find that our greatest help will come from prayer. Oh, that every Christian enterprise were commenced with prayer, continued with prayer, and crowned with prayer! Then might we also expect to see it crowned with God's blessing. So once again I remind you that our Savior's example teaches us that for seasons of special service we need not only prayers of a brief character, excellent as they are for ordinary occasions, but special protracted wrestling with God like that of Jacob at the brook Jabbok, so that each one of us can say to the Lord, with holy determination,

> With thee all night I mean to stay,
> And wrestle till the break of day.

When such sacred persistence in prayer as this becomes common throughout the whole church of Christ, Satan's long usurpation will be coming to an end, and we shall be able to say to our Lord, as the seventy disciples did when they returned to Him with joy, "Even the devils are subject unto us through thy name."

Prayer in Preparation for Transfiguration

Our Lord's prayer preparatory to His transfiguration is found in Luke 9:28–29: "And it came to pass about an eight days after these sayings, he took Peter and John and James, and went up into a mountain to pray. And as he prayed, the fashion of his countenance was altered, and his raiment was white and glistering." You see that it was as He prayed that He was transfigured.

Now, beloved, do you really desire to reach the highest possible attainments of the Christian life? Do you, in your inmost soul, pine and pant after the choicest joys that can be known by human beings this side of heaven? Do you aspire to rise to full fellowship with the Lord Jesus Christ and to be transformed into His image from glory to glory? If so, the way is open to you; it is the way of prayer, and only there will you find these priceless boons. If you fail in prayer, you will assuredly never come to Tabor's top. There is no hope, dear friends, of our ever attaining to anything like a transfiguration and being covered with the light of God, so that whether in the body or out of the body we cannot tell, unless we are much in prayer.

I believe that we make more real advance in the divine life in an hour of prayer than we do in a month of sermon hearing. I do not mean that we are to neglect the assembling of ourselves together, as the manner of some is; but I am sure that without the praying the hearing is of little worth. We must pray, we must plead with God if we are really to grow spiritually. In prayer, very much of our spiritual digestion is done. When we are hearing the Word, we are very much like the cattle when they are cropping the grass, but when we follow our hearing with meditation and prayer, we do, as it were, lie down in the green pastures and get the rich nutriment for our souls out of the truth. My dear brother or sister in Christ, would you shake off the earthliness that still clings to you? Would you get rid of your doubting and your fearing? Would you overcome your worldliness? Would you master all your besetting sins? Would you glow and glisten in the brightness and glory of the holiness of God? Then be much in prayer as Jesus was. I am sure that it must be so, and that apart from prayer, you will make no advance in the divine life; in waiting upon God you shall renew your spiritual strength, you shall mount up with wings as eagles, you shall run and not be weary, you shall walk and not faint.

Prayer in Preparation for Great Miracles

The first of our Lord's prayers preparatory to great miracles, which preceded His stilling of the tempest on the lake of Gennesaret, is recorded in Matthew 14:23–25: "And when he had sent the multitudes away, he went up into a mountain apart to pray: and when the evening was come, he was there alone. But the ship was now in the midst of the sea, tossed with waves: for the wind was contrary. And in the fourth watch of the night Jesus went unto them, walking on the sea." He had been pleading with His Father for His disciples; then, when their ship was tossed by the waves and driven back by the contrary winds, He came down to them from the lofty place where He had been praying for them, making a pathway for Himself across the turbulent waters that He was about to calm. Before He walked upon those tossing billows, He had prayed to His Father; before He stilled the storm, He had prevailed with God in prayer.

Am I to do any great work for God? Then I must first be mighty upon my knees. Is there a man here who is to be the means of covering the sky with clouds and bringing the rain of God's blessing upon the dry and barren church which so sorely needs reviving and refreshing? Then he must be prepared for that great work as Elijah was when, on the top of Carmel, "he cast himself down upon the earth, and put his face between his knees," and prayed as only he could pray. We shall never see a little cloud, like a man's hand, that shall afterward cover all the sky with blackness, unless first of all we know how to cry mightily to the Most High, but when we have done that, then shall we see what we desire. Moses would never have been able to control the children of Israel as he did if he had not first been in communion with his God in the desert and afterward in the mount. So, if we are to be men of power, we also must be men of prayer.

The other instance to which I want to refer, showing how our Lord prayed before working a mighty miracle, is when He stood by the grave of Lazarus. You will find the account of it in John 11:41–42: "Then they took away the stone from the place where the dead was laid. And Jesus lifted up his eyes, and said, Father, I thank thee that thou hast heard me. And I knew that thou hearest me always: but because of the people which stand by I said it, that they may believe that thou hast sent me." He did not cry, "Lazarus, come forth," so that the people heard it, and Lazarus heard it, until first He had prayed, "My Father, grant that Lazarus may rise from the dead," and had received the assurance that he would do so as soon as he was called by Christ to come forth from the grave.

But, brethren, do you not see that, if Christ who was so strong, needed to pray thus, what need there is for us who are so weak also to pray? If He, who was God as well as man, prayed to His Father before He wrought a miracle, how needful it is for us, who are merely men, to go to the throne of grace and plead there with importunate fervency if we are ever to do anything for God! I fear that many of us have been feeble out here in public because we have been feeble out there on the lone mountainside where we ought to have been in fellowship with God. The way to be fitted to work what men will call wonders is to go to the God of wonders and implore Him to gird us with His all-sufficient strength so that we may do exploits to His praise and glory.

Prayer in Preparation for Peter's Fall

We have the record of our Lord's prayer preparatory to Peter's fall in Luke 22:31–32: "And the Lord said, Simon, Simon, behold, Satan hath desired to have you, that he may sift you as wheat: but I have prayed for thee, that thy faith fail not: and when thou art converted, strengthen thy brethren."

There is much that is admirable and instructive in this utterance of our Lord. Satan had not then tempted Peter, yet Christ had already pleaded for the apostle whose peril He clearly foresaw. Some of us would have thought that we were very prompt if we had prayed for a brother who had been tempted and who had yielded to the temptation, but our Lord prayed for Peter before he was tempted. As soon as Satan had desired to have him in his sieve that he might sift him as wheat, our Savior knew the thought that was formed in the diabolic mind, and He at once pleaded for His imperiled servant, who did not even know the danger that was threatening him. Christ is ever beforehand with us. Before the storm comes He has provided the harbor of refuge; before the disease attacks us, He has the remedy ready to cure it; His mercy outruns our misery.

What a lesson we ought to learn from this action of Christ! Whenever we see any friend in peril through temptation, let us not begin to talk about him, but let us at once pray for him. Some persons are very fond of hinting and insinuating about what is going to happen to certain people with whom they are acquainted. I pray you, beloved friends, not to do so. Do not hint that So-and-so is likely to fall, but pray that he may not fall. Do not insinuate anything about him to others, but tell the Lord what your anxiety is concerning him.

"But So-and-so has made a lot of money, and he is getting very purse-proud." Well, even if it is so, do not talk about him to others, but pray God to grant that he may not be allowed to become purse-proud. Do not say that he will be, but pray constantly that he may not be, and do not let anyone but the Lord know that you are praying for him.

"Then there is So-and-so; he is so elated with the success he has had that one can scarcely get to speak to him." Well, then, brother, pray that he may not be elated. Do not say that you are afraid he is growing proud, for that would imply what you would yourself be if you were in his place. Your fear reveals a secret concerning your own nature, for what you judge that he would be is exactly what you would be in similar circumstances. We always measure other people's corn with our own bushel—we do not borrow their bushel—we can judge ourselves by our judgment of others. Let us cease these censures and judgments, and let us pray for our brethren. If you fear that a minister is somewhat turning aside from the faith or if you think that his ministry is not so profitable as it used to be or if you see any other imperfection in him, do not go and talk about it to people in the street, for they cannot set him right; go and tell his Master about him, pray for him and ask the Lord to make right whatever is wrong. There is a sermon by old Matthew Wilks about our being epistles of Christ, written not with ink and not in tables of stone, but in fleshly tables of the heart. He said that ministers are the pens with which God writes on their hearers' hearts, and that pens need nibbing every now and then, and even when they are well nibbed they cannot write without ink; he said that the best service that the people could render to the preachers is to pray the Lord to give them new nibs and dip them in the ink afresh that they might write better than before. Do so, dear friends; do not blot the page with your censures and unkind remarks, but help the preacher by pleading for him even as Christ prayed for Peter.

Prayer in Preparation for Death

You will find our Lord's preparatory prayer just before His death in Luke 23:46: "And when Jesus had cried with a loud voice, he said, Father, into thy hands I commend my spirit: and having said thus, he gave up the ghost."

Our Lord Jesus was very specially occupied in prayer as the end of His earthly life drew near. He was about to die as His people's Surety and Substitute; the wrath of God, which was due to them, fell upon Him. Knowing all that was to befall Him, "He steadfastly set his face to go to Jerusalem"; and, in due time, He "endured the cross, despising the shame"; but He did not go to Gethsemane and Golgotha without prayer. Son of God as He was, He would not undergo that terrible ordeal without much supplication. You know how much there is about His praying in the later chapters of John's gospel. There is especially that great prayer of His for His church, in which He pleaded with wonderful fervor for those whom His Father had given Him. Then there was His agonized pleading in Gethsemane, when His sweat "was as it were great drops of blood falling down to the ground." We will not say much about that, but we can well imagine that the bloody sweat was the outward and visible expression of the intense agony of His soul, which was "exceeding sorrowful, even unto death."

All that Christ did and suffered was full of prayer, so it was but fitting that His last utterance on earth should be the prayerful surrender of His spirit into the hands of His Father. He had already pleaded for His murderers, "Father, forgive them; for they know not what they do." He had promised to grant the request of the penitent thief. "Lord, remember me when thou comest into thy kingdom." Now nothing remained for Him to do but to say, "Father, into thy hands I commend my spirit: and having said thus, he gave up the ghost." His life, which had been a life of prayer, was thus closed with prayer—an example well worthy of His people's imitation.

Perhaps I am addressing someone who is conscious that a serious illness is threatening. Well then, dear friend, prepare for it by prayer. Are you dreading a painful operation? Nothing will help you to bear it so well as pleading with God concerning it. Prayer will help you mentally as well as physically; you will face the ordeal with far less fear if you have laid your case before the Lord and committed yourself, body, soul, and spirit, into His hands. If you are expecting, before long, to reach the end of your mortal life because of your advanced age or your weak constitution or the inroads of the deadly consumption, pray much. You need not fear to be baptized in Jordan's swelling flood if you are constantly being baptized in prayer. Think of your Savior in the Garden and on the cross, and pray even as He did, "Not my will, but thine, be done. . . . Father, into thy hands I commend my spirit."

While I have been speaking thus to believers in our Lord Jesus Christ, there may have been some here who are still unconverted, who have imagined that prayer is the way to heaven; it is not. Prayer is a great and precious help on the road, but Christ alone is the way, and the very first step heavenward is to trust ourselves wholly to Him. Faith in Christ is the all-important matter; if you truly believe in Him, you are saved. But the very first thing that a saved man does is to pray, and the very last thing that he does before he gets to heaven is to pray. Well did Montgomery write—

> Prayer is the contrite sinner's voice,
> Returning from his ways;
> While angels in their songs rejoice,
> And cry, "Behold, he prays!"

> Prayer is the Christian's vital breath,
> The Christian's native air;
> His watchword at the gates of death:
> He enters heaven with prayer.

12

The Redeemer's Prayer

Father, I will that they also, whom thou hast given me, be with me where I am; that they may behold my glory, which thou hast given me: for thou lovedst me before the foundation of the world (John 17:24).

W hen the high priest of old entered into the most holy place, he kindled the incense in his censer and waving it before him, he perfumed the air with its sweet fragrance and veiled the mercy seat with the denseness of its smoke. Thus was it written concerning him, "He shall take a censer full of burning coals of fire from off the altar before the Lord, and his hands full of sweet incense beaten small, and bring it within the vail: and he shall put the incense upon the fire before the LORD, that the cloud of the incense may cover the mercy seat that is upon the testimony, that he die not." Even so our Lord Jesus Christ, when He would once for all enter within the veil with His own blood to make an atonement for sin, did first offer strong crying and prayers. In this seventeenth chapter of John, we have, as it were, the smoking of the Savior's pontifical censer. He prayed for the people for whom He was about to die, and before He sprinkled them with His blood, He did sanctify them with His supplications. This prayer therefore stands preeminent in Holy Writ as the Lord's Prayer— the special and peculiar prayer of our Lord Jesus Christ; "if," as an old divine has it, "it be lawful to prefer one Scripture above another, we may say, though all be gold, yet this is a pearl in the gold; though all be like the heavens, this is as the sun and stars." Or if one part of Scripture be more dear to the believer than any other, it must be this which contains his Master's last prayer before He entered through the rent veil of His own crucified body. How sweet it is to see that not He Himself but

This sermon was taken from *The Metropolitan Tabernacle Pulpit* and was preached on Sunday morning, April 17, 1858.

136

His people constituted the staple of His prayer! He did pray for Himself—He said, "Father, glorify thou me," but while He had one prayer for Himself, He had many for His people. Continually did He pray for them—"Father, sanctify them!" "Father, keep them!" "Father, make them one!" And then He concluded His supplication with, "Father, I will that they also, whom thou hast given me, be with me where I am." Melancthon well said there was never a more excellent, more holy, more fruitful, and more affectionate voice ever heard in heaven or in earth than this prayer.

We shall first notice *the style of the prayer*; secondly, *the persons interested in it*; and thirdly, *the great petition offered*—the last head constituting the main part of our discourse.

The Style of the Prayer

The style of the prayer is singular: it is, "Father, *I will*." Now, I cannot but conceive that there is something more in the expression, "I will," than a mere wish. It seems to me that when Jesus said "I will," although perhaps it might not be proper to say that He made a demand, yet we may say that He pleaded with authority, asking for that which He knew to be His own and uttering an "I will" as potent as any fiat that ever sprang from the lips of the Almighty. "Father, I will." It is an unusual thing to find Jesus Christ saying to God, "I will." You know that before the mountains were brought forth, it was said of Christ, "in the volume of the book it is written of me, I delight to do *thy will*, O my God" (italics mine); and we find while He was on earth that He never mentioned His own will; He expressly declared, "I came . . . not to do mine own will, but the will of him that sent me." It is true you do hear Him when addressing men, saying "I will," for He says, "I will; be thou clean"; but in His prayers to His Father He prayed with all humility. "*I will*," therefore, seems to be an exception to the rule, but we must remember that Christ was now in an exceptional condition. He had never been before where He was now. He was now come to the end of His work; He could say, "I have finished the work which thou gavest me to do," and therefore, looking forward to the time when the sacrifice would be complete and He should ascend on high, He sees that His work is done and takes His own will back again and says, "Father, I will."

Now, mark that such a prayer as this would be totally unbecoming in our lips. We are never to say, "Father, *I will*." Our prayer is to be, "Not my will, but thine be done." We are to mention our wishes, but our wills are to subside into the will of God. We are to feel that while it is ours to desire, it is God's to will. But how pleasant, I repeat, it is to find the Savior pleading with such authority as this, for this puts the stamp of certainty upon His prayer. Whatsoever He has asked for in that chapter

He shall have beyond a doubt. At other times, when He pleaded as a mediator, in His humility He was eminently successful in His intercessions; how much more shall His prayer prevail now that He takes to Himself His great power and with authority cries, "Father, I will." I love that opening to the prayer; it is a blessed guarantee of its fulfillment, rendering it so sure that we may now look upon Christ's prayer as a promise that shall be assuredly fulfilled.

The Persons for Whom He Prayed

"Father, I will that *they also, whom thou hast given me*, be with me where I am." This was not a universal prayer. It was a prayer including within it a certain class and portion of mankind who are designated as those whom the Father had given Him. Now we are tonight to believe that God the Father did, from before the foundation of the world, give to His Son Jesus Christ a number whom no man can number, who were to be the reward of His death, the purchase of the travail of His soul; who were to be infallibly brought to everlasting glory by the merits of His passion and the power of His resurrection. These are the people here referred to. Sometimes in Scripture they are called the elect, because when the Father gave them to Christ, He chose them out from among men. At other times they are called the beloved, because God's love was set upon them of old. They are called Israel; for like Israel of old, they are a chosen people, a royal generation. They are called God's inheritance, for they are especially dear to God's heart, and as a man cares for his inheritance and his portion, so the Lord cares especially for them.

Let me not be misunderstood. The people whom Christ here prays for are those whom God the Father out of His own free love and sovereign good pleasure ordained to eternal life and who, in order that His design might be accomplished, were given into the hands of Christ the Mediator, by Him to be redeemed, sanctified, and perfected, and by Him to be glorified everlastingly. These people, and none others, are the object of our Savior's prayer. It is not for me to defend the doctrine; it is scriptural, that is my only defense. It is not for me to vindicate God from any profane charge of partiality or injustice. If there be some wicked enough to impute this to Him, let them settle the matter with their Maker. Let the thing formed, if it have arrogance enough, say to Him that formed it, "Why have You made me thus?" I am not God's apologist; He needs no defender. "O man, who art thou that repliest against God?" Hath he not, like the potter, power over the clay, to make one vessel to honor and another to dishonor? Instead of disputing, let us inquire who are these people? Do we belong to them? Oh! let each heart now put the solemn query, "Am I included in that happy throng whom God the Father gave to Christ? Beloved, I cannot tell you by the mere hearing of your names, but if I know your character, I can tell you decisively—or rather, you will need no telling, for the Holy Spirit will bear witness in your hearts that you are among the number. Answer this question—have you given yourselves to Christ? Have you been brought by the constraining power of His own free love to make a voluntary surrender of yourself to Him? Have you said, "O Lord, other lords have had dominion over me, but now I reject them, and I give myself up to You, and as I have no other refuge, so I have no other Lord. Little am I worth, but such as I am I give all I have and all I am to You. It is true I was never worth Your purchasing, but since You have bought me, You shall have me. Lord, I make a full surrender of myself to You." Well, soul, if you have done this, if you have given yourself to Christ, it is but the result of that ancient grant made by Jehovah to His Son long before the worlds were made. And, once again, can you feel today that you are Christ's? If you cannot remember the time when He sought you and brought you to Himself, yet can you say with the spouse, "I am my beloved's"? Can you now from your inmost soul say, Whom have I in heaven but You, and there is none upon earth that I desire beside You! If so, trouble not your minds about election; there is nothing troublesome in election to you. He that believes is elected; he who is given to Christ now was given to Christ from before the foundation of the world. You need not dispute divine decrees, but you may sit down and draw honey out of this rock and wine out of this flinty rock. Oh, it is a hard, hard doctrine to a man who has no interest in it, but when a man has once a title to it, then it is like the rock in the wilderness; it streams with refreshing water whereat myriads may drink and never thirst again. Well does the Church of England say of that doctrine, it "is full of sweet, pleasant, and unspeakable comfort to godly persons." And though it be like the Tarpeian rock, whence many a malefactor has been dashed to pieces in presumption, yet it is like Pisgah, from whose lofty summit the spires of heaven may be seen in the distance. Again, I say, be not cast down, neither let your hearts be disconsolate. If you be given to Christ now, you are among the happy number for whom He intercedes above, and you shall be gathered among the glorious throng, to be with Him where He is and to behold His glory.

The Petitions That the Savior Offers

Christ prayed, if I understand His prayer, for three things—things that constitute heaven's greatest joy, heaven's sweetest employment, and heaven's highest privilege.

The first great thing He prayed for is that which is *heaven's greatest joy*—"Father, I will that they also, whom thou hast given me, be with me where I am." If you notice, every word in the sentence is necessary to its fullness. He does not say—I pray that those, whom thou hast given me,

may be where I am"; but, "*with me* where I am." And He does not only
pray that they might be with Him, but that they might be with Him in the
same place where He is. And mark! He did not say He wished His people to be in heaven, but with Him in heaven, because that makes heaven
heaven. It is the very pith and marrow of heaven to be with Christ.
Heaven without Christ would be but an empty place, it would lose its
happiness, it would be a harp without strings, and where would be the
music?—a sea without water, a very pool of Tantalus. Christ prayed then
that we might be with Him—that is our companionship; with Him
where He is—that is our position. It seems as if He would tell us that
heaven is both a condition and a state—in the company of Christ and in
the place where Christ is.

I might, if I chose, enlarge very much on these points, but I just throw
out the raw material of a few thoughts that will furnish you with topics
of meditation in the afternoon. Let us now pause and think how sweet
this prayer is by contrasting it with our attainments on earth. "Father, I
will that they also, whom thou hast given me, be with me where I am."
Ah! brothers and sisters, we know a little of what it is to be with Christ.
There are some happy moments, sweet pauses; between the din of the
continued battles of this wearied life there are some soft times, like
couches of rest, wherein we do repose. There are hours when our Master
comes to us and makes us, or ever we are aware, like the chariots of
Amminadib. It is true, we have not been caught up to the third heaven
like Paul, to hear words that it is unlawful for us to utter, but we have
sometimes thought that the heavens have come down to us. Sometimes I
have said within myself, "Well, if this be not heaven, it is next door to
it," and we have thought that we were dwelling in the suburbs of the ce-
lestial city. You were in that land, which Bunyan calls the land Beulah.
You were so near to heaven that the angels did flit across the stream and
bring you sweet bunches of myrrh and bundles of frankincense, which
grow in the beds of spices on the hills, and you pressed these to your
heart and said with the spouse, "A bundle of myrrh is my well beloved
unto me; he shall lie all night betwixt my breasts," for I am ravished
with His love and filled with His delights. He has made Himself near to
me, He has unveiled His countenance and manifested all His love.

But, beloved, while this gives us a foretaste of heaven, we may nevertheless use our state on earth as a complete contrast to the state of the glorified above. For here, when we see our Master, it is but at a distance. We
are sometimes, we think, in His company, but still we cannot help feeling
that there is a great gulf fixed between us, even when we come the nearest to Him. We talk, you know, about laying our heads upon His bosom
and sitting at His feet, but alas! we find it after all to be very metaphorical
compared with the reality that we shall enjoy above. We have seen His

face, we trust we have sometimes looked into His heart, and we have tasted that He is gracious, but still, long nights of darkness lay between us. We have cried again and again with the bride, "O that thou wert as my brother, that sucked the breasts of my mother! when I should find thee without, I would kiss thee; yea, I should not be despised. I would lead thee, and bring thee into my mother's house, who would instruct me: I would cause thee to drink of spiced wine of the juice of my pomegranate." We were with Him, but still He was in an upper room of the house and we below; we were with Him, but still we felt that we were absent from Him, even when we were the nearest to Him.

Again, even the sweetest visits from Christ, how short they are! Christ comes and goes very much like an angel; His visits are few and far between with the most of us, and oh! so short—alas, too short for bliss. One moment our eyes see Him, and we rejoice with joy unspeakable and full of glory, but again a little time and we do not see Him, our beloved withdraws Himself from us; like a roe or a young hart He leaps over the mountain of division; He is gone back to the land of spices and feeds no more among the lilies. Oh, how sweet the prospect of the time when we shall not see Him at a distance, but face-to-face. There is a sermon in those words, face-to-face. And then we shall not see Him for a little time. Oh, if it is sweet to see Him now and then, how sweet to gaze on that blessed face for aye and never have a cloud rolling between and never have to turn one's eyes away to look on a world of weariness and woe! Best days! when shall you come, when our companionship with Christ shall be close and uninterrupted?

And let us remark, again, that when we get a glimpse of Christ, many step in to interfere. We have our hours of contemplation when we do draw near to Jesus, but alas! how the world steps in and interrupts even our most quiet moments—the shop, the field, the child, the wife, the head, perhaps the very heart, all these are interlopers between ourselves and Jesus. Christ loves quiet; He will not talk to our souls in the busy marketplace, but He says, "Come, My love, into the vineyard, get thee away into the villages, there will I show thee My love." But when we go to the villages, behold the Philistine is there, the Canaanite has invaded the land. When we would be free from all thought except thought of Jesus, the wandering band of Bedouin thoughts come upon us, and they take away our treasures and spoil our tents. We are like Abraham with his sacrifice; we lay out the pieces ready for the burning, but foul birds come to feast on the sacrifice that we desire to keep for our God and for Him alone. We have to do as Abraham did: When the birds came down upon the sacrifice, Abraham drove them away." But in heaven there shall be no interruption; no weeping eyes shall make us for a moment pause in our vision; no earthly joys, no sensual delights, shall create a discord in our melody; there shall we have no fields to till, no garment to spin, no wearied limb, no dark distress, no burning thirst, no pangs of hunger, no weepings of bereavement; we shall have nothing to do or think upon but forever to gaze upon that Sun of Righteousness with eyes that cannot be blinded and with hearts that can never be weary. To be in those arms forever, throughout a whole eternity to be pressed to His bosom, to feel the beatings of His ever faithful heart, to drink His love, to be satisfied forever with His favor, and to be full with the goodness of the Lord—oh! if we have only to die to get to such delights as these!—death is gain, it is swallowed up in victory.

Nor must we turn away from the sweet thought that we are to be with Christ where He is, until we have remembered that though we often draw near to Jesus on earth, yet the most we ever have of Him is but a sip of the well. We sometimes come to the wells of Elim and the seventy palm trees, but when sitting beneath the palm trees, we feel that it is just like an oasis; tomorrow we shall have to be treading the burning sands with the scorching sky above us. One day we sit down and we drink from the sweet soft spring; tomorrow we know that we have to be standing with parched lips over Marah's fount crying, "Alas, alas! it is bitter; I cannot drink thereof." But oh, in heaven, we shall do what holy Rutherford says, we shall put the wellhead to our lips and drink right on from that well that never can be drained, we shall drink to our souls' utmost full. Aye, as much of Jesus as the finite can hold of infinity shall the believer receive. We shall not then see Him for the twinkling of an eye and then lose Him, but we shall see Him ever. We shall not eat of manna that shall be like a small round thing, a coriander seed, but the manna whereof we feed shall be mountains, the broad hills of food; there we shall have rivers of delight and oceans of ecstatic joy. Oh, it is very hard for us to tell, with all that we can guess of heaven, how large, how deep, how high, how broad it is. When Israel ate of that one fair branch that came from Eshcol, they guessed what the clusters of Canaan must be, and when they tasted the honey they guessed the sweetness. But I warrant no man in all that host had any idea of how full that land was of fertility and sweetness, how the very brooks ran with honey and the very rocks did teem with fatness. Nor can any of us who have lived the nearest to our Master form more than the faintest guess of what it is to be with Jesus where He is.

Now all that is wanted to help my feeble description of being with Jesus is this—if you have faith in Christ, just think over this fact, that in a few more months you will know more about it than the wisest mortal before can tell. A few more rolling suns, and you and I shall be in heaven. Go on, O time! with your swiftest pinions fly! A few more years, and I shall see His face. O can you say, my hearer, "I shall see His face?" Come, you gray-headed one nearing the goal of life, can you with confidence say, "I know that my Redeemer liveth"? If you can say that, it will fill your soul with joy. I can never think of it without being moved to tears. To think that this head shall wear a crown; that these poor fingers shall strike the harp strings of everlasting song; that this poor lip, which now faintly tells the wonders of redeeming grace, shall join with cherubim and seraphim and rival them in melody. Is it not too good to be true? Does it not seem sometimes as if the very greatness of the thought overwhelmed our faith? But true it is; though too great for us to receive, it is not too great for God to give. We shall be with Him where He is. Yes, John; you laid your head upon your Savior's bosom once, and I have oftentimes envied you, but I shall have your place by and bye. Yes, Mary; it was your sweet delight to sit at your Master's feet while Martha was cumbered with her much serving. I, too, am too much cumbered with this world, but I shall leave my Martha's cares in the tomb and sit to hear your Master's voice. Yes, O spouse, you did ask to be kissed with the kisses of his lips, and what you asked for, poor humanity shall yet see. And the poorest, meanest, and most illiterate of you who have trusted in Jesus shall yet put your lips to the lips of your Savior—not as Judas did—but with a true "Hail, Master!" you shall kiss Him. And then, wrapped in the beams of His love, as a dim star is eclipsed in the sunlight, so shall you sink into the sweet forgetfulness of ecstasy, which is the best description we can give of the joys of the redeemed. "Father, I will that they also, whom thou hast given me, be with me where I am." That is heaven's sweetest joy, to be with Christ.

And now the next prayer is, "that they may behold my glory, which thou hast given me." This is *heaven's sweetest employment*. I doubt not there are many joys in heaven that will amplify the grand joy with which we have just started; I feel confident that the meeting of departed friends, the society of apostles, prophets, priests, and martyrs will amplify the joy of the redeemed. But still the sun that will give them the greatest light to their joy will be the fact that they are with Jesus Christ and behold His face. And now there may be other employments in heaven, but that mentioned in the text is the chief one, "That they may behold my glory." O for the tongue of angel! O for the lip of cherubim! for one moment to depict the mighty scenes that the Christian shall behold when he sees the glory of his Master, Jesus Christ! Let us pass as in a panorama before our eyes the great scenes of glory that we shall behold after death. The moment the soul departs from this body it will behold the glory of Christ. The glory of His person will be the first thing that will arrest our attention. There will He sit in the midst of the throne, and our eyes will first be caught with the glory of His appearance. Perhaps we shall be struck with astonishment. Is this the visage that was more marred than that of any man? Are these the hands once torn by rude iron? Is that the head that once was crowned with thorns? Oh, how shall our admiration rise and rise and rise to the very highest pitch, when we shall see Him who was humble and full of woes, now King of Kings and Lord of Lords. What! are those fire-darting eyes the very eyes that once wept over Jerusalem? Are those feet, shod with sandals of light, the feet that once were torn by the flinty acres of the Holy Land? Is that the Man who, scarred and bruised, was carried to His tomb? Yes, it is He. And that shall absorb our thoughts—the godhead and the manhood of Christ; the wondrous fact that He is God over all blessed forever—and yet man, bone of our bone, flesh of our flesh. And when for an instant we have noted this, I doubt not the next glory we shall see will be the glory of His *enthronement*. Oh, how will the Christian stop at the foot of His Master's throne and look upward, and if there could be tears in heaven, tears of rich delight will roll down his cheeks when he looks and sees the Man enthroned. "Oh," says he, "I often used to sing on earth, "Crown Him! crown Him! crown Him King of Kings and Lord of Lords!" And now I see Him; up those hills of glorious light my soul does not dare to climb. There, there He sits! Dark with insufferable light His skirts appear. Millions prostrate themselves with rapture. Ah! we shall not deliberate many moments, but taking our crowns in our hands we shall help to swell that solemn pomp, and casting our crowns at His feet, we shall join the everlasting song, "Unto him that loved us, and washed us from our sins in his own blood, . . . to him be glory . . . for ever and ever." Can you imagine the magnificence of the Savior? Can you conceive how thrones and princes, principalities and powers, all wait at His beck and command? You cannot tell how well the tiara of the universe does fit His brow, or how the regal purple of all worlds does gird His shoulders; but certain it is, from the highest heaven to the deepest hell, He is Lord of Lords—from the furthest east to the remotest west, He is master of all. The songs of all creatures find a focus in Him. He is the grand reservoir of praise. All the rivers run into the sea, and all the hallelujahs come to Him, for He is Lord of all. Oh, this is heaven—it is all the heaven I wish, to see my Master exalted; this has often braced my loins when I have been weary and often steeled my courage when I have been faint. "God also hath highly exalted him, and given him a name which is above every name: that at the name of Jesus every knee should bow, of things in heaven, and things in earth, and things under the earth."

And then the believer will have to wait a little while, and then he shall see more glorious things yet. After a few years, he will see the glories of the latter day. We are told in prophecy that this world is to become the dominion of Christ. At present, idolatry and bloodshed and cruelty and lusts do reign. But the hour is coming when this Augean stable shall be cleansed once and forever; when these huge shambles of

Aceldama shall yet become the temple of the living God. We believe that in these times, Christ with solemn pomp will descend from heaven to reign upon this earth. We cannot read our Bibles and believe them literally without believing that there are bright days coming when Christ shall sit upon the throne of His father David, when He shall hold His court on earth and reign among His ancients gloriously. But oh, if it be so, you and I shall see it, if we belong to the happy number who have put their trust in Christ. These eyes shall see that pompous appearance, when He shall stand in the latter day upon the earth. "Mine eyes shall behold, and not another." I could almost weep to think that I have lost the opportunity of seeing Christ on earth as crucified. I do think the twelve apostles were very highly favored, but when we shall see our Savior here, and shall be like our Head, we shall think that all deficiencies are made up in the eternal weight of glory. When from the center to the poles the harmony of this world shall all be given to His praise, these ears shall hear it; when all nations shall join the shout, this tongue shall join the shout also. Happy men and happy women who have such a hope, so to behold the Savior's glory.

And then, after that a little pause; a thousand years shall run their golden cycle, and then shall come the judgment. Christ, with sound of trumpet, in pomp terrific, shall descend from heaven—angels shall form His bodyguard, surrounding Him on either hand. The chariots of the Lord are twenty thousand, even thousands of angels. The whole sky shall be clad with wonders. Prophecies and miracles shall be as rife and as plentiful as the leaves upon the trees. The earth shall totter at the tramp of the Omnipotent; the pillars of the heavens shall stagger like drunken men beneath the weight of the eternal splendor—heaven shall display itself in the sky while on earth all men shall be assembled. The sea shall give up its dead; the graves shall yield their tenants; from the cemetery and the graveyard and the battlefield, men shall start in their thousands; every eye shall see Him, and they who have crucified Him. And while the unbelieving world shall weep and wail because of Him, seeking to hide themselves from the face of Him that sits upon the throne, believers shall come forward and, with songs and choral symphonies, shall meet their Lord. Then shall they be caught up together with the Lord in the air, and after He has said, "Come, ye blessed," they shall sit upon His throne, judging the twelve tribes of Israel; they shall take their seats as assessors upon that awful judgment bench; when at the last He shall say, "Depart, ye cursed," and His left hand shall open the door of thunder and let loose the flames of fire, they shall cry, Amen; and when the earth shall vanish and men shall sink into their appointed doom, they, gladly seeing the triumph of their Master, shall shout again, again, again the shout of victory—"Hallelujah, for the Lord God hath triumphed over all."

And to complete the scene, when the Savior shall ascend on high for the last time, His victories all completed and death himself being slain, He, like a mighty conqueror about to ride through heaven's bright streets, shall drag at His chariot wheel hell and death. You and I, attendants at His side, shall shout the victor to His throne; while the angels clap their bright wings and cry, "the Mediator's work is done." We shall behold His glory. Picture whatever splendor and magnificence you please, if you do but conceive it rightly, you shall behold it.

You see people in this world running through the streets to see a king or a queen ride through them. How they do climb to their housetops to see some warrior return from battle. Ah, what a trifle! What is it to see a piece of flesh and blood, though it be crowned with gold. But oh! what is it to see the Son of God with heaven's highest honors to attend Him, entering within the pearly gates while the vast universe resounds with "Alleluia: for the Lord God omnipotent reigneth."

I must close by noticing the last point, which is this. In our Savior's prayer heaven's greatest privilege is also included. Mark, we are not only to be with Christ and to behold His glory, but we are to be like Christ and to be glorified with Him. Is He bright? So shall you be. Is He enthroned? So shall you be. Does He wear a crown? So shall you. Is He a priest? So shall you be a priest and a king to offer acceptable sacrifices forever. Mark, that in all Christ has, a believer has a share. This seems to me to be the sum total and the crowning of it all—to reign with Christ, to ride in His triumphal chariot and have a portion of His joy; to be honored with Him, to be accepted in Him, to be glorified with Him. This is heaven, this is heaven indeed.

And now, how many of you are there here who have any hope that this shall be your lot? Well said Chrysostom, "The pains of hell are not the greatest part of hell; the loss of heaven is the weightiest woe of hell"; to lose the sight of Christ, the company of Christ, to lose the beholding of His glories, this must be the greatest part of the damnation of the lost.

Oh, you that have not this bright hope, how is it that you can live? You are going through a dark world, to a darker eternity. I beseech you stop and pause. Consider for a moment whether it is worthwhile to lose heaven for this poor earth. What! pawn eternal glories for the pitiful pence of a few moments of the world's enjoyments? No, stop I beseech you; weigh the bargain before you accept it. What shall it profit you to gain the whole world and lose your soul and lose such a heaven as this?

But as for you who have a hope, I beseech you, hold it fast, live on it, rejoice in it. Live near your Master now, so shall your evidences be bright; when you come to cross the flood, you shall see Him face-to-face, and what that is only they can tell who enjoy it every hour.

13

John's First Doxology

Unto him that loved us, and washed us from our sins in his own blood, and hath made us kings and priests unto God and his Father; to him be glory and dominion for ever and ever. Amen (Revelation 1:5–6).

John had hardly begun to deliver his message to the seven churches, he had hardly given in his name and stated from whom the message came, when he felt that he must lift up his heart in a joyful doxology. The very mention of the name of the Lord Jesus, "the faithful witness, and the first begotten of the dead, and the prince of the kings of the earth," fired his heart. He could not sit down coolly to write even what the Spirit of God dictated; he must rise; he must fall upon his knees; he must bless and magnify and adore the Lord Jesus. This text is just the upward burst of a great geyser of devotion. John's spirit has been quiet for awhile, but on a sudden the stream of his love to Jesus leaps forth like a fountain, rising so high that it would seem to bedew heaven itself with its sparkling column of crystal love. Look at the ascending flood as you read the words, "Unto him that loved us, and washed us from our sins in his own blood, and hath made us kings and priests unto God and his Father; to him be glory and dominion for ever and ever. Amen."

Now, in the matter of this bursting out of devotion at unexpected times, John is one among the rest of the apostles. Their love to their divine Master was so intense that they had only to hear His footfall and their pulses began to quicken, and if they heard His voice, then were they carried clean away. Whether in the body or out of the body, they could not tell, but they were under constraint to magnify the Savior's name; whatever they were doing they felt compelled to pause at once, to render direct

---

This sermon was taken from *The Metropolitan Tabernacle Pulpit* and was preached on Sunday morning, September 2, 1883.

and distinct homage to the Lord Jesus by adoration and doxology. Observe how Paul breaks forth into doxologies: "Now unto him that is able to do exceeding abundantly above all that we ask or think, according to the power that worketh in us, unto him be glory in the church by Christ Jesus throughout all ages, world without end. Amen." Again, "Now unto the King eternal, immortal, invisible, the only wise God, be honor and glory for ever and ever. Amen." The like is true of Jude, who cries: "Now unto him that is able to keep you from falling, and to present you faultless before the presence of his glory with exceeding joy, to the only wise God our Savior, be glory and majesty, dominion and power, both now and ever. Amen." The apostles overflowed with praise.

This explains to me, I think, those texts that bid us "rejoice evermore," "bless the Lord at all times," and "pray without ceasing." These do not mean that we are always to be engaged in devotional exercises, for that would cause a neglect of other duties. The very apostle who bids us "pray without ceasing" did a great many other things beside praying; we should certainly be very faulty if we shut ourselves up in our private chambers and there continued perpetually upon our knees. Life has other duties, and necessary ones; in attending to these we may render to our God the truest worship. To cease to work in our callings in order to spend all our time in prayer would be to offer to God one duty stained with the blood of many others. Yet we may "pray without ceasing," if our hearts are always in such a state that at every opportunity we are ready for prayer and praise, better still, if we are prepared to make opportunities, if we are instant in season and out of season and ready in a moment to adore and supplicate. If not always soaring, we may be as birds ready for instant flight, always with wings, if not always on the wing. Our hearts should be like beacons made ready to be fired. When invasion was expected in the days of Queen Elizabeth, piles of wood and combustible material were laid ready on the tops of certain hills, and watchmen stood prepared to kindle the piles should there be notice given that the ships of the enemy were in the offing. Everything was in waiting. The heap was not made of damp wood, neither had they to go and seek kindling; but the fuel waited for the match. The watch fire was not always blazing, but it was always ready to shoot forth its flame. Have you never read, "Praise waiteth for thee, O God, in Sion"? So let our hearts be prepared to be fired with adoring praise by one glimpse of the Redeemer's eyes; to be all on a blaze with delightful worship with one touch from that dear, pierced hand. Anywhere, wherever we may be, may we be clad in the robes of reverence and be ready at once to enter upon the angelic work of magnifying the Lord our Savior. We cannot be always singing, but we may be always full of gratitude, and this is the fabric of which true psalms are made.

This spontaneous outburst of John's love is what I am going to preach upon this morning. First of all I shall ask you to consider *the condition of heart out of which such outbursts come*, and then we will look more closely at *the outburst itself*, for my great desire is that you and I may often be thus transported into praise, carried off into ecstatic worship. I long that our hearts may be like eolian harps through which each wind as it sweeps on its way makes charming music. As roses are ready to shed their perfume, so may we be eager to praise God, so much delighting in the blessed exercise of adoration that we shall plunge into it when colder hearts do not expect us to do so. I have read of Mr. Welch, a minister in Suffolk, that he was often seen to be weeping, and when asked why, he replied that he wept because he did not love Christ more. May not many of us weep that we do not praise Him more? Oh, that our meditation may be used of the Holy Spirit to help us in that direction!

The Condition of Heart Out of Which
Outbursts of Adoration Arise

Who was this man who when he was beginning to address the churches must needs lay down his pen to praise the Savior? We will learn the character of the man from his own devout language. We shall see his inmost self here, for he is carried off his feet and speaks out his very heart in the most unguarded manner. We shall now see him as he is and learn what manner of persons we must be if, like him, we would overflow with praise. It would be easy to talk at great length about John from what we know of his history from other parts of Scripture, but at this time I tie myself down to the words of the text, and I notice, first, that this man of doxologies, from whom praise flashes forth like light from the rising sun, is first of all *a man who has realized the person of his Lord*. The first word is, "Unto *him*"; then he must a second time before he has finished say, "To *him* be glory and dominion." His Lord's person is evidently before his eye. He sees the actual Christ upon the throne. The great fault of many professors is that Christ is to them a character upon paper, certainly more than a myth, but yet a person of the dim past, an historical personage who lived many years ago and did most admirable deeds by the which we are saved, but who is far from being a living, present, bright reality. Many think of Jesus as gone away, they know not whither, and He is little more actual and present to them than Julius Caesar or any other remarkable personage of antiquity. We have a way, somehow, a very wicked way it is, of turning the facts of Scripture into romances, exchanging solidities for airy notions, regarding the august sublimities of faith as dreamy, misty fancies, rather than substantial matters of fact. It is a grand thing personally to know the Christ of God as a living existence, to speak into His ear, to look into His face, and to understand that we abide in Him and that He is ever with us, even to the end of the world. Jesus was no abstraction to John; he loved Him too much for that. Love has a great vivifying power; it makes our impressions of those who are far away from us very lifelike and brings them very near. John's great, tender heart could not think of Christ as a cloudy conception, but he remembered Him as that blessed One with whom he had spoken and on whose breast he had leaned. You see that is so, for his song rises at once to the Lord's own self, beginning with, "Unto him."

He makes us see Jesus in very act of which he speaks in his doxology. It runs thus: "Unto him that loved us." It is not "Unto the love of God," an attribute or an influence or an emotion; it is "Unto *him* that loved us." I am very grateful for love, but more grateful to Him who gives the love. Somehow, you may speak of love and eulogize it, but if you know it only in the abstract, what is it? It neither warms the heart nor inspires the spirit. When love comes to us from a known person, then we value it. David had not cared for the love of some unknown warrior, but how greatly he prized that of Jonathan, of which he sang, "Thy love to me was wonderful, passing the love of women"! Sweet is it to sing of love, but sanctified hearts delight still more to sing, "Unto *him* that loved us."

So, too, is it with the washing from sin. It is enough to make us sing of pardoning mercy forever and ever if we have been cleansed from sin, but the center of the joy is to adore Him "that washed us from our sins in his own blood." Observe that He cleansed us, not by some process outside of Himself, but by the shedding of His own blood of reconciliation. It brings the blood-washing into the highest estimation with the heart when we look into the wounds from whence the atonement flowed, when we gaze upon that dear visage so sadly marred, that brow so grievously scarred, and when we even peer into the heart that was pierced by the spear for us to furnish a double cleansing for our sin. "Unto him that washed us." The disciples were bound to love the hands that took the basin and poured water on their feet and the loins which were girt with the towel for their washing; we, brethren, must do the same. But as for the washing with His own blood, how shall we ever praise Him enough? Well may we sing the new song, saying, "Thou art worthy . . . , for thou wast slain, and hast redeemed us to God by thy blood." This puts body and weight into our praise when we have realized *Him* and understood how distinctly these precious deeds of love as well as the love itself come from Him whose sacred heart is all our own.

So, too, if we are "kings and priests," it is Jesus who has made us so.

> Round the altar priests confess:
> If their robes are white as snow.
> 'Twas the Savior's righteousness
> And His blood that made them so.

Our royal dignity and our priestly sanctity are both derived from Him. Let us not only behold the streams but also consider the source. Bow before the blessed and only Potentate who does encrown and enthrone us; extol the faithful high priest who does enrobe and anoint us. See the divine actor in the grand scene and remember that He ever lives, and therefore to Him should we render perpetual glory. John worships the Lord Himself. His mind is not set upon His garments, His crowns, His offices, or His works, but upon Him, His very self. "I SAW HIM," says the beloved apostle, and that vision almost blotted out the rest. His heart was all for Jesus. The censer must smoke *unto Him*, the song must rise *unto Him*—unto Him, unto His very self.

I pray that every professor here may have a real Christ, for otherwise he will not be a real Christian. I want you to recognize in this realization of Christ by John this teaching—that we are to regard our holy faith as based on facts and realities. We have not followed cunningly devised fables. Do you believe in the divine life of Christ? Do you also believe that He who is "very God of very God" actually became incarnate and was born at Bethlehem? Do you put down the union of the Godhead with our humanity as an historical fact that has the most potent bearing upon all the history of mankind? Do you believe that Jesus lived on earth and trod the blessed acres of Judea, toiling for our sakes, and that He did actually and really die on the behalf of sinners? Do you believe that He was buried and on the third day rose again from the dead? Are these stories in a book or facts in the life of a familiar friend? To me it is the grandest fact in all history, that the Son of God died and rose again from the dead and ever lives as my representative. Many statements in history are well attested, but no fact in human records is one-half as well attested as the certain resurrection of Jesus Christ from the dead. This is no invention, no fable, no parable, but a literal fact, and on it all the confidence of the believer leans. If Christ is not risen, then your faith is vain; as He surely rose again and is now at the right hand of God, even the Father, and will shortly come to be our judge, your faith is justified and shall in due season have its reward. Get a religion of facts and you will have a religion that will produce facts by operating upon your life and character, but a religion of fancies is but a fancied religion, and nothing practical will come of it.

To have a real, personal Christ is to get good anchor-hold for love and faith and hope. Somehow men cannot love that which is not tangible.

That which they cannot apprehend they do not love. When I was about to commence the orphanage at Stockwell, a gentleman who had had very large experience in an excellent orphanage said to me, "Begin by never expecting to receive the slightest gratitude from the parents of the children, and you will not be disappointed"; for, said he, "I have been connected with a certain orphanage," which he mentioned, "for a great many years, and except in the rarest case, I have never seen any tokens of gratitude in any of the mothers whose children have been received." Now, my experience is very different. I have had a great many grips of the hand that meant warm thanks, and I have seen the tears start from the mothers' eyes full often, and many a grateful letter have I received because of help given to the orphan children. How do I explain the difference? Not that our orphanage has done more than the other, but the other orphanage is conducted by a committee with no well-known head, and hence it is somewhat of an abstraction; the poor women do not know who is to be thanked and, consequently, thank nobody. In our own case the poor people say to themselves, "Here is Mr. Spurgeon, and he took our children into the orphanage." They recognize in me the outward and visible representative of the many generous hearts that help me. They know me, for they can see me, and they say, "God bless you," because they have someone to say it to. There is nothing particular about me, certainly, and there are others who deserve far more gratitude than that which comes to me, but it does come to me because the poor people know the name and the man and have not to look at a mere abstraction. Pardon the illustration; it suits my purpose well. If you have Christ whom you cannot realize, you will not love Him with that fervent affection that is so much to be desired. If you cannot reach the Lord in your mind, you will not embrace Him in your heart, but if you have realized the blessed Master, if He has become a true existence to you, one who has really loved you and washed you from your sins and made you a king and a priest, then your love must flow out toward Him. You cannot resist the impulse to love one who has so truly loved you and is so well known to you.

This also gives foothold to faith. If you know the Lord Jesus, you feel that you can trust Him. "They that know thy name will put their trust in thee." Those to whom Christ has become a well-known friend do not find it difficult to trust Him in the time of their distress. An unknown Christ is untrusted, but when the Holy Spirit reveals Jesus, He also breeds faith. By the same means, your hope also becomes vivid, for you say, "Oh, yes, I know Jesus, and I am sure that He will keep His word. He has said, 'I will come again and receive you unto myself,' and I am sure that He will come, for it is not like Him to deceive His own chosen." Hope's eyes are brightened as she thinks of Jesus and realizes

Him as loving to the end; in Him believing, she rejoices with joy unspeakable and full of glory. To love, to trust, to hope are all easy in the presence of a real living Christ, but if, like the disciples at midnight on the Galilean lake, we think Him to be a mere specter or apparition, we shall be afraid and cry out for fear. Nothing will suffice a real Christian but a real Christ.

Next, the apostle John, in whom we note this outburst of devotion, was a man *firmly assured of his possession* of the blessings for which he praised the Lord. Doubt has no outbursts; its chill breath freezes all things. Oh, for more assurance! Nowadays we hear Christian people talk in this way, "Unto Him that we hope has loved us, and that we humbly trust has washed us, and that we sometimes believe has made us kings, unto Him be glory." Alas! the doxology is so feeble that it seems to imply as little glory as you like. The fact is, if you do not know that you have a blessing, you do not know whether you ought to be grateful for it or not, but when a man knows he has covenant mercies, that divine assurance that the Holy Spirit gives to Christians works in him a sacred enthusiasm of devotion to Jesus. He knows what he enjoys, and he blesses Him from whom the enjoyment comes. I would have you, beloved, know beyond all doubt that Jesus is yours, so that you can say without hesitation, "He loved me and gave Himself for me." You will never say, "Thou knowest all things; thou knowest that I love thee," unless you are first established upon the point that Jesus loves you, for "we love him, because he first loved us." John was certain that he was loved, and he was furthermore most clear that he was washed, and therefore he poured forth his soul in praise. Oh, to know that you are washed from your sins in the blood of Jesus! Some professors seem half afraid to say that they are cleansed, but hearer, if you are a believer in Jesus, the case is clear, for "there is therefore now no condemnation to them which are in Christ Jesus"! He that believeth in Him hath everlasting life. He that believeth in Him is justified from all things from which he could not be justified by the law of Moses. "Ye are clean," says Christ. "He that is washed needeth not save to wash his feet, but is clean every whit: and ye are clean."

> O how sweet to view the flowing
>   Of the Savior's precious blood!
> With divine assurance, knowing
>   He has made my peace with God.

This well-grounded assurance will throw you into ecstasy, and it will not be long before the deep of your heart will well up with fresh springs of adoring love. Then shall you also praise the Lord with some such words as these: "Unto him that loved us, and washed us from our sins in his own blood, . . . to him be glory and dominion for ever and ever. Amen."

I think we have brought out two points that are clear enough. John had realized his Master and firmly grasped the blessing that his Master brought him, but *he had also felt*, and was feeling very strongly, *his communion with all the saints*. Notice the use of the plural pronoun. We should not have wondered if he had said, "Unto him that loved *me*, and washed *me* from my sins in his own blood." Somehow there would have been a loss of sweetness had the doxology been so worded, and it would have hardly sounded like John. John is the very mirror of love, and he cannot live alone or rejoice in sacred benefits alone. John must have all the brotherhood round about him, and he must speak in their name, or he will be as one bereft of half himself. Beloved, it is well for you and me to use this *us* very often. There are times when it is better to say *me*, but in general let us get away to the *us*; for has not our Lord taught us when we pray to say, "Our Father which art in heaven. Give us this day our daily bread; forgive us our trespasses," and so on? Jesus does not bid us say, "My Father." We do say it, and it is well to say it, but our usual prayers must run in the "Our Father" style, and our usual praises must be, "Unto him that loved *us*, and washed *us* form our sins." Let me ask you, beloved brethren, do you not love the Lord Jesus all the better and praise Him all the more heartily because His grace and love are not given to you alone? Why, that blessed love has embraced your children, your neighbors, your fellow church members, myriads who have gone before you, multitudes that are round about you, and an innumerable company who are coming after; for this we ought to praise the gracious Lord with unbounded delight. It seems so much the more lovely—this salvation, when we think of it not as a cup of water of which one or two of us may drink, but as a well of water opened in the desert, ever flowing, ever giving life and deliverance and restoration to all who pass that way. "Unto him that loved us." Oh, my Lord, I bless You for having loved me, but sometimes I think I could adore You for loving my wife, for loving my children and all these dear friends around me, even if I had no personal share in Your salvation. Sometimes this seems the greater part of it, not that I should share in Your compassion, but that all these poor sheep should be gathered into Your fold and kept safe by You. The instinct of a Christian minister especially leads him to love Christ for loving the many, and I think the thought of every true worker for the Lord runs much in the same line. No man will burst out into such joyful adoration as we have not before us unless he has a great heart within him, full of love to all the brotherhood; then, as he looks upon the multitude of the redeemed around about him, he will be prompted to cry with enthusiastic joy:

> To him that lov'd the souls of men,
>   And wash'd us in his blood,
> To royal honors raised our head,
>   And made us priests to God;
>
> To him let every tongue be praise,
>   And every heart be love!
> All grateful honors paid on earth,
>   And nobler songs above!

Thus much upon the condition of heart that suggests these doxologies.

The Outburst Itself

It is a doxology, and as such does not stand alone: *it is one of many.* In the book of the Revelation doxologies are frequent, and in the first few chapters they distinctly grow as the book advances. If you have your Bibles with you, as you ought to have, you will notice that in this first outburst only two things are ascribed to our Lord. "To him be glory and dominion for ever and ever." Now turn to the fourth chapter at the ninth verse, and read, "Those beasts give glory and honor and thanks to him that sat on the throne." Here we have three words of honor. Run on to verse eleven, and read the same. "Thou art worthy, O Lord, to receive glory and honor and power." The doxology has grown from two to three in each of these verses. Now turn to chapter 5:13, "And every creature which is in heaven, and on the earth, and under the earth, and such as are in the sea, and all that are in them, heard I saying, Blessing, and honor, and glory, and power, be unto him that sitteth upon the throne, and unto the Lamb for ever and ever." Here we have four praise notes. Steadily but surely there is an advance. By the time we get to chapter 7:12, we have reached the number of perfection and may not look for more. "Blessing, and glory, and wisdom, and thanksgiving, and honor, and power, and might, be unto our God for ever and ever. Amen." If you begin praising God, you are bound to go on. The work engrosses the heart. It deepens and broadens like a rolling river. Praise is somewhat like an avalanche; it may begin with a snowflake on the mountain moved by the wing of a bird, but that flake finds others to itself and becomes a rolling ball; this rolling ball gathers more snow about it until it is huge, immense; it crashes through a forest; it thunders down into the valley; it buries a village under its stupendous mass. Thus praise may begin with tears of gratitude; anon the bosom swells with love; thankfulness rises to a song; it breaks forth into a shout; it mounts up to join the everlasting hallelujahs that surround the throne of the Eternal. What a mercy it is that God by His Spirit will give us greater capacities by and by than we have here! For if we continue to learn more and more of the love of

Christ, which passes knowledge, we shall be driven to sore straits if con-
fined within the narrow and drowsy framework of this mortal body. This
poor apparatus of tongue and mouth is already inadequate for our zeal.

> Words are but air and tongues but clay,
> But his compassions are divine.

We want to get out of these fetters and rise into something better adapted
to the emotions of our spirit. I cannot emulate the songsters of
Immanuel's land though I would gladly do so; as Berridge says—

> Strip me of this house of clay,
> And I will sing as loud as they.

These doxologies occur again and again throughout this book as if to remind us to be frequent in praise, and they grow as they proceed, to hint
to us that we also should increase in thankfulness.

Now, this outburst *carried within itself its own justification*. Look at it
closely and you perceive the reasons why, in this enthusiastic manner,
John adores his Savior. The first is, "Unto him that *loved* us." Time
would fail me to speak long on this charming theme, so I will only notice briefly a few things. This love is in the present tense, for the passage
may be read, "Unto him that loveth us." Our Lord in His glory still loves
us as truly and as fervently as He did in the days of His flesh. He loved
us before the world was; He loves us now with all His heart, and He will
love us when sun and moon and stars have all expired like sparks that
die when the fire is quenched upon the hearth and men go to their beds.
"He loveth us." He is Himself the same yesterday, today, and forever,
and His love is like Himself. Dwell on the present character of it and be
at this moment moved to holy praise.

He loved us first before He washed us, "Unto him that loved us, and
washed us," not, "Unto him that washed us and loved us." This is one of
the glories of Christ's love, that it comes to us while we are defiled with
sin—yes, dead in sin. Christ's love does not only go out to us as washed,
purified, and cleansed, but it went out toward us while we were yet foul
and vile and without anything in us that could be worthy of His love at
all. He loved us and then washed us; love is the fountainhead, the first
source of blessing.

Think of this as being a recognizable description of our Lord—"Unto
him that loved us." John wanted to point out the Lord Jesus Christ, and
all he said was, "Unto him that loved us." He was sure nobody would
make any mistake as to whom was intended, for no one can be said to
love us in comparison with Jesus. It is interesting to note that, as John is
spoken of as "that disciple whom Jesus loved," so now the servant de-
scribes the Master in something like the same terms, "Unto him that

loved us." No one fails to recognize John or the Lord Jesus under their several love names. When the apostle mentioned "him that loved us," there was no fear of men saying, "That is the man's friend or father or brother." No, there is no love like that of Jesus Christ; He bears the palm for love; yes, in the presence of His love all other love is eclipsed, even as the sun conceals the stars by His unrivaled brightness.

Again, the word "him that loved us" seems as if it described all that Christ did for us, or, at least, it mentions first the grandest thing He ever did, in which all the rest is wrapped up. It is not, "Unto him that took our nature; unto him that set us a glorious example; unto him that intercedes for us"; but, "Unto him that loved us," as if that one thing comprehended all, as indeed it does.

He loves us; this is matter for admiration and amazement. Oh, my brethren, this is an abyss of wonder to me! I can understand that Jesus pities us; I can very well understand that He has compassion on us; but that the Lord of glory loves us is a deep, great, heavenly thought, which my finite mind can hardly hold. Come, brother, and drink of this wine on the lees, well refined. Jesus loves you. Grasp that. You know what the word means in some little degree according to human measurements, but the infinite Son of God loved you of old, and He loves you now! His heart is knit with your heart, and He cannot be happy unless you are happy.

Remember, He loves you with His own love according to His own nature. Therefore He has for you an infinite love altogether immeasurable. It is also, like Him, immutable and can never know a change. The emperor Augustus was noted for his faithfulness to his friends, whom he was slow in choosing. He used to say, "Late ere I love, long ere I leave." Our blessed Lord loved us early, but He never leaves us. Has He not said, "I will never leave thee, nor forsake thee"? The love of Jesus is a pure, perfect, and divine love, a love whose heights and depths none can measure. His nature is eternal and undying, and such is His love. He could not love you more; He will never love you less. With all His heart and soul and mind and strength He loves you. Come; is not that a grand excuse, if excuse is wanted, for often lifting up our hearts and voices in hearty song to the Lord? Why should we not seven times a day exult before Him, saying, "Unto him that loved us, and washed us from our sins in his own blood, and hath made us kings and priests unto God and his Father, to him be glory and dominion for ever and ever. Amen"? Oh, for new crowns for His blessed brow! Oh, for new songs for His love-gifts ever new! Praise Him! Praise Him, all earth and heaven!

Then the apostle passes on to the second reason why he should thus magnify the Lord Jesus by saying, "And washed us from our sins in his own blood." "Washed us." Then we were foul; He loved us though we were unclean. He washed *us* who had been more defiled than any. How could He condescend so far as to wash *us?* Would He have anything to do with such filthiness as ours? Would that sublime holiness of His come into contact with the abominable guilt of our nature and our practice? Yes, He loved us so much that He washed us from our sins, black as they were. He did it effectually, too: He did not try to wash us, but He actually and completely washed us from our sins. The stains were deep and damnable; they seemed indelible, but He has "washed us from our sins." No spot remains, though we were black as midnight. "Wash me, and I shall be whiter than snow" has been realized by every believer here. But think of how He washed us—"with his own blood." Men are chary of their own blood, for it is their life; yet will brave ones pour it out for their country or for some worthy object; but Jesus shed His blood for such unworthy ones as we are, that He might by His atonement forever put away the iniquity of His people. At what a cost was this cleansing provided! Too great a cost I had almost said. Have you never felt at times as if, had you been there and seen the Lord of glory about to bleed to death for you, you would have said, "No, my Lord, the price is too great to pay for such a one as I am"? But He has done it; brethren, His sin-atoning work is finished forever. Jesus has bled, and He has washed us, and we are clean beyond fear of future defilement. Shall He not have glory for this? Will we not wish Him dominion for this?

> Worthy is he that once was slain,
> The Prince of Peace that groan'd and died;
> Worthy to rise, and live, and reign
> At his Almighty Father's side.

Does not this doxology carry its justification in its own bowels? Who can refuse to praise at the remembrance of such grace as this?

Nor is this all. The Lord that loved us would do nothing by halves, and therefore when He washed us in His own blood, He "made us kings." What is that? Are we kings this morning? We do not feel our crowns as yet nor perhaps grasp our scepters as we might, but the Lord has made us a royal priesthood. We reign over our own selves, and that is a dominion which is hard to gain, indeed, impossible without grace. We walk like kings among the sons of men, honored before the Lord and His holy angels—the peerage of eternity. Our thoughts, our aims, our hopes, and our longings are all of a nobler kind than those of the mere carnal man. Ours is a nature of a higher order than theirs, since we have been born again of the Spirit. Men know us not because they know not our Lord, but we have a heritage they have not, and we have prepared for us a crown of life which fades not away. The Lord has made us kings and endowed us with power before His presence; yes, He has made us rich since all things are ours. We read of the peculiar treasures of kings, and we have choice wealth of grace. He has made us even now among the sons of men to possess the earth and to delight ourselves in the abundance of peace.

Furthermore our Lord has made us priests. Certain men impiously set up to be priests above the rest of the Lord's people. As Korah, Dathan, and Abiram are they, and they had need fear lest they and their evil system should go down into the pit. Whoever they may be, all the people of God are priests. Every man that believes in Jesus Christ is from that moment a priest, though he be neither shaven nor shorn nor bedecked in peculiar array. To the true believer his common garments are vestments, every meal is a sacrament, every act is a sacrifice. If we live as we should live, our houses are temples, our hearts are altars, our lives are an oblation. The bells upon our horses are holiness to the Lord, and our common pots are as the bowls before the altar. It is the sanctification of the Holy Spirit that gives men a special character so that they are the priesthood of the universe. The world is dumb, and we must speak for it; the whole universe is as a great organ, but it is silent; we place our fingers on the keys, and the music rises toward heaven. We are to be priests for all mankind. Wherever we go we are to teach men and to intercede with God for them. In prayer and praise we are to offer up acceptable oblations, and we are ourselves to be living sacrifices, acceptable to God by Jesus Christ our Lord. Oh, what dignity is this! How you and I are bound to serve God! Peter Martyr told Queen Elizabeth, "Kings and queens are more bound to obey God than any other persons; first as God's creatures, and secondly as His servants in office." This applies to us also. If common men are bound to serve God, how much more those whom He has made kings and priests to His name!

What does the doxology say? "To him be glory and dominion." First, "To him be glory." Oh, give Him glory, my beloved, this morning! Do I address any that have never yet accepted Christ's salvation? Accept it now and thus give your Savior glory. Have you never trusted Jesus to save you? The best, the only thing you can do to give Him glory is to trust Him now, sinner as you are, that He may remove your transgressions. Are you saved? Then, dear brother, give Him glory by speaking well of His name and by perpetual adoration. Glorify Him in your songs, glorify Him in your lives. Behave yourselves as His disciples should do, and may His Spirit help you.

But the doxology also ascribes to Him dominion. My heart longs for Jesus to have dominion. I wish He might get dominion over some poor heart this morning that has hitherto been in rebellion against Him! Yield you, rebel! Yield to your Sovereign and Savior! "Kiss the Son, lest he be angry, and ye perish from the way, when his wrath is kindled but a little." To Him be dominion over hearts that have never submitted to Him. Reign, my Lord, reign in my bosom more and more; cast out every enemy and every rival; reign supreme, and reign eternally. Set up Your throne also more and more conspicuously in the hearts and lives of all who call themselves Christians. O my brethren, ought it not to be so? Is it not clear to you that since He has loved and washed us, He should have dominion over us? Ah! let Him have dominion over the wide, wide world, until they that dwell in the wilderness shall bow before Him, and His enemies shall lick the dust. Reign forever, King of Kings and Lord of Lords.

Then it is added, let Him have glory and dominion "for ever and ever." I suppose we shall have some gentlemen coming up to prove that "for ever and ever" only means for a time. They tell us that everlasting punishment means only for a time, and, of course, everlasting life must mean just the same, and this praise must also have a limit. I mean not so, nor do you, beloved. I pray that our Lord may have endless glory over this generation and the next and the next until He comes, and then that it may be said, "The Lord shall reign for ever and ever." Hallelujah! As long as there is wing of angel or son of man, as long as God Himself shall live, may the Lord Jesus Christ that loved us and washed us have glory and dominion.

Now we have come to the last word of the text. It finishes up with "Amen." "For ever and ever. Amen." Can you heartily say "Amen" to this? Do you wish Christ to have glory and dominion forever and ever? If you know He loved you, I am sure you do; if you know He washed you, I am sure you do. Now let your beating hearts in solemn silence say, "Amen"; and when we have done that, do you think you could join with one voice with me and say it out aloud, like thunder? Now, "Unto him that loved us, and washed us from our sins in his own blood, and hath made us kings and priests unto God and his Father, to him be glory and dominion for ever and ever. Amen," and "Amen" yet again. (Here the great congregation joined aloud with the preacher.) The prayers of David the son of Jesse were ended when he came to that, and so may ours be, and so may this morning's service be. God bless you through His adorable Son. Amen and Amen.